The Diary of
PIERRE LAVAL

Pierre Laval upon his arrival in New York in 1931

The Diary of
PIERRE LAVAL

With a Preface

By

JOSÉE LAVAL

Countess R. de Chambrun

CHARLES SCRIBNER'S SONS · NEW YORK

1948

PREFACE TO THE AMERICAN EDITION

IN HIS LAST LETTER my father wrote me: "I shall disappear from this world; mingle with the earth which swallows us all; but my soul shall live on and will never leave you. I shall always be at your and your mother's side, so that you may never lose courage. I ask you not to dream of avenging me but, since you need not blush on my account, you may defend my memory. Do so calmly, without rancor and in the certainty that, with the return to a just order of things, I shall once more find my place in the hearts of good men. Face misfortune standing erect. All France knows now that I was deliberately prevented from speaking and defending myself. Later, she will exact an explanation and an accounting. Mine they would not listen to. May my sacrifice at least serve those who have suffered unjustly or who are threatened because they, too, wanted to serve their country in her hours of misfortune."

Those words have given me the courage to write this Preface.

You are not going to read memoirs. A man of action like my father, a statesman such as he was, does not write memoirs. He leaves that to conscientious observers, witnesses of the acts they will write into history. Or else it is left to the culpable, the prevaricators, who seek to justify their political mistakes. They will present the history of their day, trying always to appear in the best light themselves. Such books flourish especially after such periods as we have just passed through. You will find nothing of that in the pages ahead. My father wrote them in prison, on the narrow board he used as a desk, in a cell crawling with vermin, with only his memory to draw on, in our unhappy France of 1945.

"I had asked for the Journal Officiel,* in order that the French might know the charges and my replies. It was refused. It was unnecessary for France to know her own history," he wrote bitterly, on the last page he left.

* Pierre Laval, as customary in important cases, had asked that the record of his trial be transcribed in the Official State Records.

v

He wrote these notes on odd bits of paper I had sent him. He put them down for use during the interrogations of the pre-trial examinations which never took place, to shout them in the faces of Judge and Jury had there been a real trial. He sent them back to me by his lawyers, to be typed, so that he could correct them. It was thus the manuscript of this book was pieced together.

You will find a little of everything in it. Many subjects are touched upon because the charges did not stop at anything, no matter how low or contemptible. You will note the accelerating tone of the account. At first we hear a man answering an absurd list of charges. He takes his time. Confined, deprived of all contact with the outside world (the provisional Government had seized all his papers), he goes over all the problems. Then, as event succeeds event with increasing rapidity, he replies to two counts of the indictment, then to three, and finally to nine all at once. Fully aware of the political trading of which his life was the stake, he wrote me then: "My case is not a trial but a political problem. I must be wrong so that they can be right."

Here is the climax of the drama.

I wonder if these pages will serve to recall to you my father's life during the past thirty years?

Who, during those years and before the defeat, protected your interests best?

Who, as legal defender of the Trade Unions and even of the anarchists, was the most generous and talented protector of the lowly and humble?

Who, later on, brought about the most important reform of our time: Social Insurance?

Who was always ready to face the risk of unpopularity and to assume the responsibilities of public office when others evaded them?

Who, in order to assure peace to your hearths and homes, forged the Stresa Front and the ring around Germany from Rome to Moscow?

And who, after the Popular Front had come to power, broken the Franco-Italian Alliance, thrown Mussolini into

Hitler's arms, disrupted French production and destroyed all the fruits of my father's patient labors, who was it that returned to the Government then, when disaster had overtaken us, as the receiver in a bankruptcy he had foreseen and labored to avert, in order to try to reduce the sufferings of the French people?

Do you remember the political struggles before the war?

Who, at that time, fought my father's economic and financial policies more bitterly than did Premier Léon Blum, whose life my father was later to save? The same Léon Blum who, despite his past as an undeviating militant Socialist, only last year attempted to introduce those same economic and financial measures advocated by my father twelve years before.

It was in watching my father in daily life and action, watching his courage nothing could daunt, seeing him deny himself any part in the myriad little cowardly compromises which would have earned him an easy popularity, that most of those near him came to understand the path of duty.

When, in November 1942, I learned of the American landing in North Africa, I left for Chateldun that night. There are moments in life when every minute, every word, every gesture is etched into the memory of those who experience them. Such moments are rare.

We were in the dining-room, my parents, my husband and myself. It was four o'clock in the morning. My father was preparing to leave for Munich, where he was to hand Hitler France's refusal of the offer of Military Alliance. Not knowing whether he should return, he put on the table the important documents he always carried with him. (Three times during the two years after that we were to watch him do the same thing.) I begged him then to leave the Government. He refused. I tried to convince him that his presence there would no longer serve any useful purpose. He answered that I did not understand the situation. The Germans will become harder and their toughness and their demands will grow with their military reverses, he told me. "To leave now would be to desert. I must stay here to protect the 700,000 prisoners on leave from their camps, the refugees, the Alsace-Lorrainers, the Jews, the Communists, the Free-masons. If I leave, I shall change France overnight into one vast 'Maquis.' How many thousands of French will then pay with their lives for such cowardice? Look," he said to me, "at what is happening in Poland, in the Balkans, every-where."

From that moment I measured the full extent of the sacrifice he had decided to make for his country. I know you will gauge it yourselves in reading this book.

These pages are those of a man who never knew hatred, who knew no offensive words, who did everything to avert the irreparable, who made every effort to bridge the gap of misunderstanding between peoples.

They are the pages of a Christian man, of a Christian judged by pseudo-Christians, of a European silenced by a provisional France, of a Frenchman assassinated because he had served his country too well.

The foregoing may seem too passionate to some of you, but have we not just passed through a period of passion? Passion in my father to remain in the Government from a sense of duty; passion in his assassins in their haste to stifle the voice they feared; passion in me, who lived through it all.

You who knew him, public servants of every rank and of whatever origin, all you who, like him, did not hesitate to serve France through her dark days and who have had to suffer for it, you will see that his last thought was of you.

And you, who did not suffer too much from the storm, you will judge according to your consciences, your preju-dices, opinions and preferences. But whatever those prefer-ences, I believe you will find in these pages reasons for faith and hope because, if you love democracy and really believe in it, you will meditate on the lessons to be drawn from the life of this son of Auvergne, hard-headed, indus-trious, stubborn, who, without compromising and by his intelligence and courage alone, raised himself to the peak of self-denial and sacrifice.

Josée de Chambrun

CONTENTS

APPENDICES

ILLUSTRATIONS

STATEMENT MADE BY PIERRE LAVAL'S ATTORNEYS: ME. JACQUES BARADUC AND ALBERT NAUD, MEMBERS OF THE PARIS BAR.

PRESIDENT PIERRE LAVAL was shot on October 15, 1945 without trial. The day after his death, and only then, were we given his written answers to the last charges of the Act of Accusation, which answers constitute the final chapters of this book. This fact alone shows with what undue haste the pre-trial hearings, the trial and the execution were conducted.

Upon his return to France, Pierre Laval asked the President of the Bar to designate two barristers who would assist him in preparing his defense.

On August 22nd, 1945, we held our first conversation with Pierre Laval. Up to that time neither of us had known him. At this first contact, and after hearing the disclosures he made to us, we realized at once the nobility and importance of our task.

The day before seeing Pierre Laval, we called upon President Bouchardon and upon M. Beteille, the examining magistrate. Both informed us that the case would be a very long one: after two examinations in September, the pre-trial hearings were to start in October and to be continued in November. M. Beteille handed us a schedule which called for at least twenty-five hearings.

Only four hearings ever took place; on August 23rd and on September 6, 8 and 11th, the fifth hearing was interrupted owing to the late hour and was never resumed.

On September 12th, we read in the newspapers that the pre-trial hearings had been terminated. A week later, Pierre Laval was hastily questioned about the Antilles, the Merchant Marine, the fate of the "Agneau Mystique," Max Dormoy's murder in Montelimar and the assault upon M. de Menthon on the shores of the lake of Annecy.

Although accused of "conspiracy against the internal security" of the State and of "relations with the enemy," President Laval was never examined with reference to his part at the National Assembly, nor on the reasons and circumstances of his return to power during the Occupation, nor on his negotiations with the German government, nor on the militia, nor still less on the circumstances of his departure from Paris on August 17, 1944.

Pursuant to the statute creating the High Court of Justice, the names of eighteen jurors from the "Resistance" and of eighteen jurors who were members of Parliament were to be drawn by lot from a list of jurors chosen fifty from members of Parliament and fifty from the "Resistance."

The selection of the jury was to take place October 3rd. On that day only eighteen jurors, members of Parliament, instead of fifty, appeared in Court. This in effect was a mandatory appointment rather than an impartial selection of jurors. During this public hearing, President Mongibeaux stated that the proceedings in Court must start and be completed before the general election.

The following day, the case was heard in our absence. In fact, we had asked the President of the Bar to relieve us of our task, as it had been made impossible for us to assist our client. We had never been shown the documents upon which the accusation was based, nor had we been given time to call our witnesses. Our own files were not completed.

In spite of these impossible conditions, the Presiding Judge asked us to be present in Court.

On the day after, October 5th, we appeared and pleaded that the trial be adjourned, pointing out to the Court how impossible it would be to assure the accused a fair trial without an opportunity for adequate preparation of his defense. Our motion was overruled and the proceedings continued.

On Saturday, October 6th, Pierre Laval attempted to read aloud a copy of the letter he had previously written to the Minister of Justice. Blazing with indignation at the refusal he met, he again insisted upon reading it.

Following the reading of this letter, the incidents occurred which are known the world over, incidents that made it perfectly clear that the accused was being judged by magistrates who had condemned him before trial.

Faced with the partiality, the insults and the threats of his judges, President Laval declared:

"A judicial crime is about to be perpetrated. I am ready to be the victim of this crime. I refuse to be a party to it."

He left the Court and, in his absence, as well as in ours, the Court proceeded with the hearing of "three witnesses for the prosecution."

On Monday, October 8th, two hours before the opening of the hearing set for that day, the Minister of Justice, M. Teitgen, asked us to call at his office and sent a car to fetch us. The meeting lasted over an hour. He urged us repeatedly to return to the bar, informing us that the magistrates of the examining committee had been very much impressed by Pierre Laval's answers and by his attitude. If we would agree to appear in Court again, he offered to pledge his word that "the members of the High Court would cease to threaten and insult our client."

A little later, with the complete approval of President Laval, we made known our refusal to President Mongibeaux and Attorney General Mornet, stating that the honor and the prestige of our profession prevented us from participating in proceedings which were judicial in name only.

The Presiding Judge and the Attorney General told us at that time that in urging us to agree, despite the absence of our client, at least to be present at the bar, with empty files, and without any possibility of intervening in the hearings, they were complying with the express order of General de Gaulle.

Our consciences as free men, our respect for the traditions of our profession, and our sense of justice prevented us from complying with such a request.

The next day, Tuesday, October 9th, Pierre Laval was sentenced to death without having been permitted to present his defense.

JACQUES BARADUC
ALBERT NAUD

The Diary of
PIERRE LAVAL

CHAPTER 1

PIERRE LAVAL'S POLITICAL CAREER *

Prison of Fresnes,
11 *September* 1945.

M R. PRESIDENT,
During my hearing yesterday you handed me the
Act of Accusation filed on 13 June 1945, during my
absence from France.

I wish to thank you for this communication. It has enabled me to know the charges brought against me. They consist in two accusations: first, to have threatened the internal security of the State; second, to have had relations with the enemy in time of war. I hasten to set forth in writing my immediate reactions to this document.

I am at last in a position to reply to each one of these charges. Certain of them could never have been formulated had there been any hearings. I shall be able to reply to these charges during the course of the pre-trial inquiry without any difficulty and shall prove that they are not based on any concrete reality.

I believe in your good faith and am certain that you wish

* Under French law, political cases begin by pre-trial hearings. Twenty-five hearings had been scheduled in the case of Pierre Laval. The Act of Accusation (Appendix I) was handed to him at the Fresnes Prison on 10 September 1945. The first charge read as follows:

'The career of Laval before the war began in the parties of the Left, which later repudiated him. He was several times a Minister, twice Prime Minister, and his personal fortune followed the course of his political fortune.'

Pierre Laval replied to this charge on 11 September by the hitherto unpublished letter which comprises Chapter I. This letter was delivered to the presiding Judge by Pierre Laval's attorneys on the following day, when the Provisional Government suddenly ordered the immediate termination of the pre-trial hearings.

3

to bring into the open this case which has come before you. The fact that in the past I occupied the highest posts of the Government and the further fact of my role during the occupation period, as well as the reasons which have prompted the Government to bring me before the High Court of Justice, all give to my case a quality of historical importance which must be evident to you. I have not only the right to defend myself; it is my duty to bring out in this trial the historical sequence of events during a period in which I was called upon to occupy high office, and at a time when our country suffered deep wounds.

I have nothing to fear and welcome full light on all these events; I shall give you every assistance in bringing the facts into the open, because like any honest man I welcome justice founded on truth.

The accusation begins with a charge the truth of which I cannot admit. It is this: *'Having had his origins in the parties of the Left, he was repudiated by them.'*

This charge implies that I was removed from the Socialist Party, to which I belonged. I can prove without the shadow of a doubt that I left this party of my own free will and that four years after I had resigned, the Socialist candidates, after a discussion of the situation initiated by Jean Longuet, agreed in 1924 to adopt my platform and policy. Previous to this I had publicly stated that I would no longer belong to the Socialist Party nor to any other political party.

I might add that as long as I belonged to the Socialist Party I accepted its rules of discipline. Specifically in 1917 I declined to participate in the Clemenceau Ministry as Under-Secretary of the Interior. I refused Clemenceau's proposal because he had asked me to offer to the Socialist Party a large measure of participation in his government, and the party turned down the proposal.

In 1919 I was not in agreement with my Socialist comrades. Nevertheless, because I had been elected to office by them in 1914, I preferred to stand by my political friends and run on a party label which had no chance of being accepted,

rather than agree to the offer which had been made to me
to head the national block, which was overwhelmingly successful at the elections.

The truth is that I left the Socialist Party at the end of
1920 of my own free will. I resigned when the party split
into the Socialist and Communist parties.

At this point I should like to recall that from 1914 until
last year I was continuously elected Deputy and Mayor of
Aubervilliers and an administrative decree was necessary to
take this office away from me. This occurred a year ago and
thus a twenty-year relationship between the workers who
are electors in this town and myself was brought to an end.

I might add that in October 1935, when elections to the
Senate were last held, despite the drastic economic and
financial measures I had enacted, I was elected (and there
are very few precedents for this) in two departments: the
Seine and the Puy de Dôme. This election, which was far to
the Left, was a prelude to the final victory of the Popular
Front. You will see from all this, Mr. President, that the
Left parties, in the secrecy of the ballot box, never repudiated me on the fateful days of the elections when the individual elector is master of our fate.

People who do not know me may have had certain doubts.
It seems quite clear, nevertheless, that my name cannot be
placed upon the 'renegades' list,' which, as everyone knows,
includes certain important personalities.*

In a few words I have refuted this first charge of the accusation against me, but I have not completed as yet my full
thought on this subject.

I should like to say at once that I have retained a memory
of my youth as a militant member of the extreme Left not
only because it was the time of my youth, but because, in
those days, I was surrounded by an enthusiasm, an impar-
tiality, a generosity which I never again found in any other
environment. This youth of mine left an indelible impres-

* The reference here is to Clemenceau and Briand, who both began
their careers in the Socialist Party.

sion upon me: a love of peace and a love and respect for the workers, for the little people of the world, and for true liberty.

Later on, I shall have occasion to develop at length the history of my efforts to preserve peace. This I shall do with special enthusiasm because the accusations which are made against me stress as a special crime my attitude in the period before the war. As for my devotion to workers and to humble people I believe that I proved repeatedly by deeds that I always had their interest at heart. I should like to cite in particular my sponsorship of the law providing for family insurance and the law providing for social insurance, which I was able to have enacted despite the general hostility of Parliament. Perhaps I need not mention as well the innumerable conflicts in which workers were involved and which I was able to settle. I shall mention, just to give you a specific example, the great textile strike in the North in which 150,000 working men were involved.

As for liberty, I suffered from its loss more than any other during the occupation period. Not only because I consider liberty our most precious heritage but also because it was plain to me from the outset that nothing permanent can be built under the threat of force.

This same charge which I am now answering states among other things that I was several times a member of the Government and twice Prime Minister. This is of course true. From the year 1925 I held successively practically every ministerial post. I was the collaborator of such men as Painlevé, Aristide Briand, Tardieu, Doumergue, and Flandin. Moreover, I was not only twice but three times Prime Minister (without counting my post as Head of the Government during the occupation).

Do you really believe, Mr. President, that in peace-time, in the full light of day, in the watchful presence of Parliament and of a free Press, I could have remained so long in office and returned so often to office if I had been unworthy of this trust? Do you honestly believe that M. Doumergue, as President of the Republic, or M. Doumer, would have asked me to form and head a government at that time if they had had any shadow of doubt as to my being fully endorsed by Parliament and by public opinion? Is it logical to suppose that President Lebrun, who never cared much for me, would have turned to me in 1935 had he had any doubt as to my fitness for the role and my acceptability to the country? It is true that at that time many of the party leaders carefully avoided the unpleasant responsibility and the thankless task of saving the franc.

I never hesitated, when the welfare of our country was at stake, to assume the risk and to expose myself to bitter ingratitude and unpopularity. In truth, from this time date the campaigns which were unleashed against me and which have gathered force in subsequent years. Strangely enough, it is from this time that my political adversaries began to show an interest in my personal fortune, which according to your charge 'followed the course of my political fortune.'

I am extremely surprised to find in a legal document an accusation which up to this time I have seen only in certain newspapers, notably certain sensational publications issued exclusively for campaign purposes and for the sake of political polemics.

I need not tell you that I am very proud of my humble beginnings. In the past I never bothered to reply to this form of attack because I held it in supreme contempt. I was not the least affected by, and of course not the least bit embarrassed by, the efforts of some of my political opponents to cast doubt on the origins of my personal fortune. Had I taken this accusation more seriously I should have been in a position to furnish the appropriate explanations and to prick the bubble of a mysterious myth. It will be easy for me to answer this charge. I shall confine myself at this point to a word of protest against this groundless accusation.

I conclude from this section of the 'accusation' that I am supposed to have amassed my capital by taking advantage of my privileged position as a person holding office. I have always felt that a certain ease, a modicum of means, is a guarantee of political independence in a public officer. I have never heard it suggested that men in public life should not look after their personal affairs when these are not in conflict with the interests of the State. You may be surprised to learn that I was so scrupulous on this score that I consistently refused to appear in court against the State and against the City of Paris because I was member of Parliament and a representative of the Department of the Seine. I shall surprise you less, as you are a veteran judge, when I tell you that my respect for the independence and dignity of the judicial office has consistently been so great that from the day when I was Keeper of the Seals (Minister of Justice) I never again appeared in court as a lawyer. It was not that honourable precedents were lacking for such appearances; but I felt that to refrain from appearing was the right and honourable course and I preferred to look elsewhere for my means of livelihood.

I defy anyone to show that at any time during the course of my public life I took advantage of any office to increase my estate. Apparently you have an expert's report. I have not seen it. It was drawn up in my absence from France. I have not been heard with regard to it. But you can be certain that in any event I shall reply specifically and concretely to any question which this report may raise. If it is true that I was guaranteed against want (and I shall inform you of all the details of my personal fortune) would it not be fairer and perhaps more generous and just to weigh against this the sacrifices which I made in the interests of my country when, as so many others did or would have done had they been in my place, I could have lived the rest of my life happily and in peace surrounded by my loved ones?

You will pardon me, Mr. President, if I write to you at this great length, but I wished, upon learning of the charges against me, to reply at once to the first item of the accusation. I shall reply to the others with equal directness as they come up during the further pre-trial hearings.

CHAPTER 2

RELATIONS WITH GREAT BRITAIN

I GAVE up my office as Prime Minister in January 1936 of my own free will. Customarily, a Prime Minister tenders his resignation, together with that of his ministers, to the President of the Republic after he has met with an adverse vote in one of the Chambers and after having appealed for a vote of confidence. If the wording of the accusation means what it says, I was overthrown after the question of confidence was raised on a point of foreign policy, specifically that of the Hoare-Laval plan.

This charge, as stated, is patently false. I was not interpellated in January 1936. In December 1935, on the 27th and 28th to be accurate, I was interpellated on this question and I received, after a debate which lasted two days and one night, when the question of confidence was raised, a majority vote of twenty-two in my favour.

M. Yvon Delbos interpellated me and he was supported by Paul Reynaud, de Monzie, Campinchi, Léon Blum, Gabriel Péri, Marcel Déat, and several others. It was a major parliamentary debate which was reported widely in the Press of the entire world. It was generally believed that my Government would be defeated in the final vote. I was confident of a success. This success I obtained after an exhaustive discussion of my policies and, as just stated, my majority was twenty-two votes. This was an impressive result, especially against the background of the forecasts of my political adversaries, and above all in view of the diversity and the high quality of my opponents.

Nevertheless, three weeks later, I decided to abandon office. This was after a visit to Geneva, where I met Mr. Eden. I informed the British Foreign Minister of my decision. He seemed greatly surprised and had the courtesy to express his regret at my decision to leave office.

Circumstances arise when the head of a government should feel it his duty to retire, more especially when he is at the same time Minister of Foreign Affairs. That is the case when, in his opinion, he lacks the necessary political support to assure the success of his policies. It becomes especially necessary when he finds that he is in disagreement with certain ministers whose collaboration is essential.

At that time I held the view that the support of the Radical Party was indispensable to the success of my policy. I was of the opinion that I could not remain without the full collaboration of President Herriot, then Minister of State. I had had evidence that, in the final vote of confidence accorded my Government, the Radical Party divided and that M. Herriot, who had approved the decrees formulated for the purpose of saving the franc and in order to prevent a rise in the cost of living, had disapproved of my foreign policy. To his mind I had not taken a strong enough stand in the application of sanctions against Italy. He had not seen his way to accord me his signature for the prorogation of special powers generally known as full powers, and I knew that in these circumstances my programme, the objects of which were to restore financial stability and to increase production, was doomed to failure.

I knew, moreover, that the sanction, generally known as the 'oil sanction' against Italy, was greatly desired by extreme Left elements in France and in England. I could not consider the application of this measure because I was convinced that it would lead to war, and I wished to avoid war. I held the belief, moreover, that the very same men who were combating my programme would, if they came to power and had to assume responsibility, be moved by the same fears as I was.

At all events, I resigned and I cannot refrain from observing that the oil sanction was never even suggested, and still less applied, by any of my successors. On the contrary, several weeks after I left office, Germany refortified and reoccupied the Rhineland. Normally, this violation of the Treaty of

Versailles should have been countered by the immediate application of the sanctions provided for by the Treaty of Locarno. These, however, were not applied. One speech was made and a few articles appeared in the Press, that was all.

It is therefore untrue to say, as the accusation states, that I was overthrown, and that, as a consequence of a development which never took place, I hated England and the French Parliament. I might also point out that it was not my business to mix in the internal policy of Great Britain, and that I could hardly complain of a French Parliament which, on a question of confidence, had given me a majority. The Government which succeeded me might have borne a grudge against the British Cabinet which refused to intervene when the Germans remilitarised the Rhineland, but as for me, I had no such grounds for complaint against the British Government. I was no longer in office at the time of the Rhineland affair, and never during all the time when I was in office did I have to solve a problem so delicate and so grave for the security of France.

I am not at all hesitant in giving you my views regarding Great Britain. I have not now, nor have I ever had, a feeling of resentment against that country. I have had, in the course of my governmental service, difficulties with one British Cabinet or another; and there have been many times when I was in complete agreement with the British ministers. I have always admired the tenacity with which they defend the interests of their country, notably when they believe that these interests are threatened. I have always believed that the true basis of understanding between France and England was one of mutual respect. I have never thought that successful relations with Great Britain could be based on an accord where France is in a position of inferiority to Great Britain. My personal relations with the successive British ministers were always courteous, and very often, even when I was not in complete agreement with them, my relations with them were extremely cordial. I might specifically mention my intercourse with Mr. Eden. In fact, if I might be permitted to express a wish, it would be that French ministers should serve French interests as British ministers serve British interests, no matter what their political affiliations are. They have, to the highest degree, pride of race and devotion to their traditions and to their Empire. They are, in the highest sense of the word, masters of the world. I have always had, and always shall have, for our country, no matter what vicissitudes it may now suffer, a like ambition. Those who know me well must understand that I have never, during my career, thought differently. From time to time I have had to check either the Anglomania or the Anglophobia professed by certain Frenchmen, but I have always appreciated the fact that these feelings, on the part of the French people, were ephemeral. The unity between France and Great Britain must be founded on a perfectly balanced equality of rights and it is only under these conditions that it will endure.

I shall now cite a few salient facts regarding my relations, as Minister of Foreign Affairs and as Head of the Government, with the British Government.

In 1931, at the height of the great financial crisis, I received, in the middle of the night, at his urgent request, Sir Ronald Campbell, British Chargé d'Affaires in the absence of Lord Tyrrell, the Ambassador. After hearing him I agreed, without reference to my Cabinet, for fear of an indiscretion which might affect British credit adversely, to make available the following morning from the French Treasury on a temporary loan basis the sum of three billions in gold. The coffers of the Bank of England were bare. Payments would have had to be suspended had it not been for the immediate and unstinted assistance of France. Sir Ronald Campbell thanked me with sincere emotion and said, taking my hands in his, 'M. le Président, I thank you. My country will never forget.' *

* In an Introduction written for the people of Great Britain, Josée Laval refers to this specific event (see Appendix II). See also the secret Campbell documents (Appendices II A, B, C, D, E).

In 1934 and 1935, working at Geneva in closest contact with Mr. Eden, the British delegate, I had to solve many grave and delicate problems, such as the plebiscite in the Saar and the Council Resolution regarding the assassination of King Alexander of Yugoslavia at Marseilles. My attitude and my activity were approved by Parliament and—a step for which there was no precedent—I was congratulated and thanked by name in a resolution unanimously voted by the Senate. I mention this because I wish to stress that I should not have had this success at Geneva had it not been for the loyal support of the British delegation. Occasionally, our views differed, which was perfectly normal when grave and vital questions were involved, but these differences were invariably surmounted by the exercise of mutual goodwill.

Again, in 1935, when I was informed that the Home Fleet had passed through the Straits of Gibraltar and entered the Mediterranean and was asked by the British Ambassador what the attitude of my country would be if the implementation of the sanctions policy provoked an armed conflict between Great Britain and Italy, I replied that Great Britain might count upon the immediate and unqualified support of the armed forces of France, on land, at sea, and in the air.

I have searched history to find a precedent in which a representative of France so engaged his country to support Great Britain without the binding tie of a military alliance. This precedent I have not found.

In this connection, here is the text of my report to our Parliament, in reply to a question of M. Yvon Delbos, on my negotiations with the British Government.

'In conformity with paragraph 3 of Article 16 of the Pact, I did not hesitate to pledge France's aid to Great Britain, on land, at sea, and in the air, in the event of her being attacked by Italy in the course of carrying out the sanctions policy. Moreover, in order to dissipate any uncertainty which may still exist, I wish to confirm here publicly this assurance which I gave to the British Am-

bassador in Paris and which I confirmed to Sir Samuel
Hoare during his passage through Paris.

'In connection with what has just been discussed I am
going to reveal to you a secret which normally would not
be made public because of its highly confidential nature.
I refer to our staff conversations.

'On 10 October a memorandum was received from the
British regarding the necessity of Franco-British co-operation and the utility of a contact between the General
Staffs. My comment to the Minister of the Navy was that
these technical conversations should be preceded by political agreements.

'The original feeler came on 10 October. On 18 October
I gave the political imprimatur, in a word, the undertaking
which binds, not the General Staffs, but the Government.
There followed British *notes verbales* on the 14th, 16th,
18th, and 24th. The purpose of these notes was to formal-
ise the agreements entered into under Article 16.

'Immediately thereafter the technical conversations took
place, specifically between the British Admiralty and our
Naval Ministry in the Rue Royale.

'Following the exchange of notes, the French Government dispatched to London on 30 October a detailed
memorandum. The British reply to the French memorandum was received on 2 November. Beginning 8 November
numerous exchanges took place between the two Ad-
miralties. On 9 and 10 December the conversations were
widened to include the army and air staffs.

'Gentlemen, I shall tell you something else in confidence: France, which in the person of its plenipotentiary
you abused with such eloquence on the ground that she
had betrayed Geneva, is the sole nation among the whole
fifty-four to accept obligations with the implementing
technical accords which I have just described to you.'

I am not surprised to learn that this particular number of
the *Journal Officiel* has been removed from public sale by

block purchase at the source. The clear-cut nature of my policy is perhaps to-day a cause of embarrassment to those who wished to defeat my internal policy of financial reconstruction.

The Chamber of Deputies, after my reply to M. Yvon Delbos and many others, gave me a vote of confidence. In fact, I should have had an even greater majority had I then been able to make public certain salient facts regarding my negotiations with Italy, notably the secret military accord to which I referred for the first time during the Pétain trial and which Marshal Badoglio confirmed in a statement to the Press immediately following my testimony.

I completely disagreed with the British Government when, without our knowledge, it negotiated and signed a naval agreement with the German Government. Not long before —this was in early February 1935—I visited London as Minister of Foreign Affairs, together with M. Flandin, who was then Prime Minister, and on this occasion it was agreed that thereafter neither France nor Great Britain would approach Germany separately, especially when questions relating to the rearmament of that country were involved. Therefore, when I read in the newspapers of the signing of the Anglo-German naval pact I summoned Sir George Clark, British Ambassador in Paris, and expressed to him my regret that his Government should have negotiated an agreement of this nature with Germany without consulting us. I pointed out, moreover, that this was directly contrary to the solemn pledge entered into on 4 February 1935.

I also differed with the British Government when Germany violated the military clauses of the Versailles Treaty.

The German violation of the military clauses was not, as was remilitarisation of the Rhineland, a subject for sanctions under the Locarno Pact. It constituted, however, a grave threat to our security. We discussed the issue at Stresa first of all, and later at Geneva, and I succeeded in persuading Sir John Simon to agree to the Resolution, platonic though it was, which was subsequently voted by the Council of the League of Nations.

The previous year, when the Doumergue Government was in power, Germany had proposed to increase its armed forces to 300,000 men. M. Barthou accepted this figure, but M. Tardieu and M. Herriot, in full agreement with M. Doumergue, rejected it. The British then made it plain that in their view we were mistaken to reject this German proposal. As a consequence, we did not receive a very encouraging response from the British when we asked them to join with us in protesting against the violation by Germany of the military clauses of the Versailles Treaty. Admittedly, this was on the eve of Britain's decision to conclude the naval pact with Germany to which I have referred above.

We could not, at that time, in Geneva, contemplate sanctions against Germany. We could not have commanded a majority at the League of Nations unless we were in full agreement with Great Britain. Thus our discussions at Stresa were exceedingly acute. I invited Mr. MacDonald, faced as we both were with the danger of a German war becoming more and more inevitable, to link the chain with Moscow. The Rome agreements and the Franco-Soviet Pact, which I signed, had eliminated difficulties which were said to be insurmountable. But England was not then prepared to adopt the policy of encirclement of Germany which I advocated. This policy alone would have prevented war by isolating Hitler.

In general, when the facts of British policy in Europe in the period following the Versailles Treaty are known, it can be said that my difficulties with the British were precisely the same as those which troubled my predecessors. There was one high-water mark during this period. This was when Austen Chamberlain directed the Foreign Office and signed the Locarno Treaty with Briand. In my prison cell I re-read Mr. Chamberlain's book, which emphasises the large part British interest played in inspiring these negotiations. I was not surprised or shocked to learn this; my feeling was the

opposite, because treaties are effective as instruments only in
so far as they correspond with the national interests of the
respective parties. The policies of that time were cast in a
mould far different from that of the so-called Munich Pact,
which I never approved.

I shall have completed my refutation of the false and unjust accusation that I 'hated' England because of the Ethiopian affair, when I give the facts, by way of reply, with
regard to the Hoare-Laval plan.

I stressed these details at some length in the course of my
testimony in the Pétain trial, but I wish to emphasise certain
features here.

All the attempts at Geneva to solve the Ethiopian crisis by
friendly means had successively failed. It was clear that a
peaceful solution of the crisis hinged exclusively on complete agreement between France and Great Britain.

Neither Italy nor Ethiopia would have been able to oppose
a compromise imposed by our two countries. Sir Samuel
Hoare understood this, and, with an acute sense of realities
and a desire to put an end to an adventure which threatened
to have the gravest consequences for the whole of Europe,
agreed to discuss and elaborate a formula, which I was certain Italy would accept, and which he was certain the Negus
would accept, and which we both were sure Geneva would
not oppose.

At this critical juncture there was a leak to the Press, and
market-place polemics immediately ensued. A question was
put in the House of Commons, and Sir Samuel Hoare was
forced to leave the Government. (It should be added that he
returned to the Government several days later in another
post.)

I have always regretted profoundly that this plan was not
put into effect. It has never crossed my mind that I should
bear any special grudge against England for the failure of
the plan. In fact, across the Channel, as here, public opinion
was divided. The opposition was more acute in England
than here because, in addition to the anti-fascists, whose

counterpart was the sole attacking force here, there were those who believed that the route to India was threatened. In a word, once more the English were out to defend a national interest which they believed was menaced. These are the normal fluctuations of international politics. In consequence, I had no reason to 'hate' England. I merely regretted the failure of the 'Hoare-Laval Plan', a failure which was to throw Italy step by step into the arms of Germany, to deprive France and England of the indispensable manœuvring ground of the Balkan Peninsula and bring down on our unfortunate country nothing but unhappiness. I am profoundly surprised to find at this date, in an accusation as serious as this, such an ill-founded charge, which wholly ignores and warps the recent history of our country.

CHAPTER 3

RELATIONS WITH ITALY

IN 1934, when I succeeded M. Barthou as Minister of Foreign Affairs, I began negotiations with the Soviet Government and Italy. Two important questions had to be settled with Italy. Of these, only the one concerning our colonial difficulties in Africa was followed by the public.

Italy had complained bitterly that she had not been given a fair deal under the Versailles Treaty. Her contention was that Great Britain had agreed to what she called 'her legitimate claims', but that France had turned these down.

I agreed that Italy should receive the 114,000 square kilometres constituting the Tibesti region in exchange for the cancellation of rights in Tunisia. Tibesti is marked on the maps of Africa by a blank. In the entire sector there is not a single inhabitant nor a single tree, but only sand and stones.

We were at that time very much hampered by the various types of privileges which Italy was entitled to in Tunisia. Children born of Italian parents retained Italian nationality; there were Italian schools, fishing rights along the coasts, &c. . . . Tunisia meant to the Italian people what Alsace-Lorraine means to the French. Thus, one can measure the sacrifice which Mussolini made when he renounced all these Italian privileges in Tunisia.

When the extent of Mussolini's concessions became known at the Palais Farnese (the French Embassy in Rome), I was surprised to hear important officials state their dissatisfaction and add: 'If we had a Parliament, Mussolini would be overthrown.' I remember that, at the time, M. Peyrouton, our Governor in Tunisia, reported that in the Italian schools the teachers had removed from the walls the pictures of

Mussolini and thrown them on the ground, and that the children spat upon them. I instructed M. Peyrouton to prevent the newspapers from commenting upon these demonstrations.

With reference to Ethiopia, I urged Mussolini not to resort to force. My last words to him were: 'Follow the example of Marshal Lyautey.' He committed the blunder of going to war. He started war against my will and despite my solemn protest.

I had made with Italy another agreement much more important than the treaty settling our colonial differences; I had made a real military alliance. Secret military agreements which were never publicly referred to were signed by General Gamelin and General Badoglio. Secret agreements were also signed by General Vallin, the Italian Air Minister, and General Denain, the French Air Minister. The purpose of these military agreements was precise: to defend Italy and France against a German invasion of Austria. This Treaty was of paramount importance; as long as Italy was France's ally we had a bridge leading to all those countries of Western and Eastern Europe which were then our allies. We could therefore not only benefit by whatever military strength Italy represented, but also by the added strength of Yugoslavia, Czechoslovakia, Poland, and Rumania.

Then came the period of the application of sanctions, and the wave of anti-fascism which developed in France and elsewhere. This was most unfortunate, for the anti-fascist feeling was to become stronger than the desire to preserve peace. I attempted to reconcile France's obligations to the League of Nations with a policy which would obviate a rupture with Italy that in turn would expose Tunis to attack. What I sought to do was to preserve a working agreement with Italy which would keep her on France's side in the event of a grave crisis in Europe. The copies of the correspondence from October 1935 to January 1936 are held under seal and the official texts are contained in a sealed envelope presumably in the archives of the Quai d'Orsay where I deposited them when I left office on 28 January 1936. These will show that my relations with Mussolini during this whole period were exceedingly complex, exceedingly difficult, and at times exceedingly stormy.

At this point I feel that I should put on record my dealings with Italians during the period which came after my leaving office. On innumerable occasions I received distinguished Italians who were passing through Paris, and the successive Italian Ambassadors maintained with me, until the outbreak of war, friendly but formal relations.

Among my many visitors I shall mention two as examples. First, I should like to name Senator Purricelli, a friend of the King of Italy, and to a lesser extent of Mussolini. He called at my office several times in order to express his regret at the troubled relations between our two countries. For instance, he visited me once at my home at Chateldon when my other guest was M. Labrousse, to-day a member of the Consultative Assembly. He came another time to tell me how heartbroken he was that his country was allied with Germany, and he pleaded for a reconciliation between France and Italy.

Senator Purricelli was a strong advocate of a return to the policy of 1935. He said that this might be brought about on very favourable conditions and he begged me to go to Rome, or elsewhere in Italy, for a meeting with Mussolini. He added that he had authority to make this proposal. Thereupon I saw the Italian Ambassador, with whom I maintained polite contacts as a private citizen. He said that the Italian Government's views in no way coincided with the oratorical fireworks of which unauthorised agitators were guilty. But as I was not in the Government at the time I made it quite clear to the Ambassador that I could not serve as an intermediary in this sort of negotiation. I informed M. Daladier, who was Prime Minister, of this feeler when I met him at the Senate. My desire to break the ties between Germany and Italy was so great that I went so far as to offer my services if Daladier wished to employ me, at my own risk and peril, and with the understanding that he could repudiate me if I should fail and take the credit if I should succeed.

M. Daladier replied that he would think this over and give me his reply two days later; that was on a Monday. He evidently did not wish to take advantage of this opportunity, for I never heard from him again in the matter and as a consequence I took no further action with regard to Signor Purricelli's trial balloon. Parenthetically, a reference to this may be found in the record of the secret session of the Senate, March or April 1940.

To sum up, I had no need for intermediaries had I felt it desirable to establish relations with the Italian Government.

I might give one more example of the type of contact I had. Count Arduini-Feretti was a member of the Italian colony in Paris whom I knew less well than Senator Purricelli. The Count claimed to be very pro-French and I believe that he was sincere in this. He made it a practice to call on me upon his return from each of his visits to Italy, especially during the period of hostilities between France and Germany, before Italy declared war on France. His opinions were close to those of Senator Purricelli and he, too, regretted Italy's alliance with Germany. On 9 June 1940 he rushed to me, obviously in a tense state of emotion, saying that he had just returned from Rome, that Italy was about to declare war, that there was still a possibility of avoiding this fatal step, and that if the worst came to the worst there was, as a last resort, a possibility that Mussolini might be dissuaded from attacking France. He then made certain specific suggestions and begged me to transmit them to the French Government.

I asked him whether these suggestions might be regarded as official. He told me that they originated with Baron Aloisi, formerly chief of Cabinet to Mussolini, with whom I had negotiated at Geneva when he was the Italian delegate. This type of approach is normal in diplomacy, especially in Italian diplomacy, and I was given to understand that the feeler had its real origin with Mussolini.

I at once informed General Denain, who, as Minister of

Air, had signed the agreements with his Italian counterpart in 1936 and asked him to inform President Lebrun. The President rushed him off to M. Paul Reynaud, who did nothing about it.

I left Paris this same day, that is 9 June 1940, the day Italy declared war, and Count Arduini-Feretti had the imprudence to attempt to complete his mission by calling at the Quai d'Orsay and was promptly interned as an Italian subject.

Thus, on two separate occasions when I was not in office, I was concerned with events which touched upon France's relations with Italy.

In each instance I followed the dictates of my conscience and did what I considered my duty in informing at once the French Government of what had taken place, and I left to the Government the responsibility of determining what action, if any, should subsequently be taken.

I have nothing to conceal. My purpose on these occasions was clear and I am confident in stating that my action was above reproach. Nothing that I said or did can justify the sly insinuation, contained in the Accusation, that I had some hidden purpose, namely, that I wished to bring about a change of regime in France. I state flatly in reply to this sort of stab in the back that there could be no question of confusing an activity which related exclusively to the domain of our country's foreign policy with obscure internal political objectives.

Senator Purricelli was one of the foremost contractors in Europe and he built most of the Italian autostrades. He also had business in several foreign countries and I recall that he mentioned to me at one time a plan for an autostrade across the Polish corridor. He had a higher interest in this than a material one and hoped, through the road, to diminish the danger of conflict between Poland and Germany which ultimately was to plunge Europe into war. Hitler gave his approval in principle to this project as did also the Polish authorities. I have a recollection that the project broke down owing to the fact that the Poles retracted when

Hitler put up the initial deposit of fifty million Reichsmarks.

I cite these facts merely to indicate that the Senator was a person of some consequence who had the friendliest feelings for France. He also had drawn up plans for an auto-tunnel between France and Italy in the region of Mont Blanc. Quite voluntarily—I never asked him what his political views might be—he volunteered one day that he had no great sympathy for the form of government then prevailing in Italy.

In the case of Count Arduini-Feretti, I am not certain whether or not he had Fascist sympathies. He never discussed this with me and I had an impression that his main concern, inspired by the fact that he had business interests in both countries, was to maintain friendly relations between Italy and France. At all events, he did not hesitate to denounce the militaristic adventures of Mussolini and also the alliance with Germany.

I give these facts in detail as the most convincing answer to the baseless accusation that 'from the outbreak of war Laval busied himself with attempts to negotiate peace, thanks to his relations with Mussolini.'

CHAPTER 4

THE ARMISTICE OF 1940:
THE FIRST ALLIED VICTORY?

I WISH to stress the fact that I had no part in the armistice of 1940 and that I was not in a position to take any decision or responsibility concerning it. I was not a member of the Government which asked for the armistice. Any opinion expressed by me upon the subject was a personal one which I shared, at that time, with practically all French people. Moreover, such a demand for an armistice could be formulated only in accordance with the advice and opinion, clearly enunciated, of the responsible military leaders that the continuation of the fight was impracticable, indeed impossible, and that the continuation of hostilities would mean for France a greater disaster than the armistice itself. Such was, in fact, the opinion of both General Weygand and Marshal Pétain. I was not a member of the Government. The only persons who could make a responsible decision based on the known facts were the ministers. The records of the Pétain trial clearly show that the armistice was decided upon before the arrival of the Government at Bordeaux. As for me, I had had no contact with Marshal Pétain during a long period before this. I was at my home at Chateldon when these events took place and I went to Bordeaux from Chateldon only after the decision had been made and well after the Government reached Bordeaux.

I know, of course, that my name was included in the list of ministers proposed by Marshal Pétain to President Lebrun. Obviously this had no connection with any opinion which I may have held with regard to the necessity for an armistice, which had already been decided on. I am thoroughly convinced in this connection that M. Paul Reynaud's successor, had he been anyone other than Marshal Pétain,

would also have included my name on his list. I had been
many times a minister and several times Prime Minister
during the most critical periods, such as those of 1931, 1932,
1935. (It would seem that whenever there was a critical
period I was called upon to fill the breach.) I had had a long
experience as Minister of Foreign Affairs. I had played a
responsible role in many international negotiations, and it
therefore seemed perfectly normal, in this most critical hour
in our history, to call upon me to participate in the Government. Moreover, at that time, presumably, the Marshal
believed that my association with him would be useful in
view of my long experience in governmental posts. Another
consideration, borne out by the Accusation brought against
me in 1946, was the fact that I had not participated in the
Government which had requested and signed the armistice.
I had refused the portfolio of Minister of Justice in the
Pétain Government, taking into consideration M. Charles
Roux' negative advice; the Marshal did not confer upon
me the post of Minister of Foreign Affairs, already assigned
to M. Baudouin. At long last, and after much discussion, I
was asked to share with M. Camille Chautemps the post of
Vice-President of the Council of Ministers.

From that time forward and up to 10 July 1940, I played,
according to the Act of Accusation, a preponderant role.
Here, I presume, we have reached one of the most important
charges against me; in any case, it is the first which can be
considered as justifying the charge that I conspired against
the internal security of the State.

In order that I may reply clearly and pertinently I must
cite the fifth charge, which includes and emphasises the
previous accusation levelled against me and which is based,
falsely of course, on my supposed role in the request for an
armistice.

This fifth charge reads as follows:

*'He bears without a doubt the greatest responsibility,
as a result of his intrigues and of his threats which reached*

even into the immediate entourage of the President of the Republic, for the fact that the President of the Republic, the presidents of the two Chambers, the members of Parliament and those ministers who still had any thought for the national sovereignty, failed to proceed to North Africa where they might have formed a government removed from the immediate threat of German reprisals and which, before Europe and America, might suitably have represented France and affirmed the continuation of its sovereign role among the nations.'

I was accused of responsibility for an armistice in which I could not possibly have any part, and now I am blamed and made responsible for an action in which I had absolutely no part at all. I could stop short here and rest on this statement. But in so doing I should appear to be washing my hands of a decision which, personally as a Frenchman, even if not as a Minister, I regarded as necessary when it was taken. This does not mean that I should have been ready to accept the armistice in the form in which it was presented to us at Rethondes. It has been said that the armistice was imposed upon us, that it could not be discussed, and that our plenipotentiaries had to accept it as it stood, when they were faced with the German victors. I have never been prepared to accept this explanation. To me it always seemed, and still seems to-day, that the representatives of France should have protested solemnly against those clauses of the Armistice Convention which rendered it *inapplicable*.

In actual fact it was the application of these clauses of the armistice which suffocated our country and made it impossible for it to have any normal life. Our representatives might at least have registered their protests or at least have recorded their observations, and this should have been done at the time and on the day of the armistice in order that discussions and negotiations might have been undertaken afterwards to clarify and interpret the implementation of this document of surrender.

It was inevitable that there would be discussions and interpretations in the days, months, and years which followed, but as matters stood and without the advantage of the protest which should have been made, every attempt at compromise with regard to the armistice served henceforward as a pretext for further demands from the Germans and a call for further sacrifices from the French. This, I repeat, was due to the fact that no reservations were made on our part at the time the armistice document was signed. *Had I been in the Government at that time I should have insisted upon having, if nothing better could have been obtained, at least a protocol outlining the conditions under which the armistice was to be applied.*

Before dwelling at length on the alleged intrigues in which I was said to be engaged and the threat I was supposed to have uttered in the very office of the President of the Republic, threats and intrigues whose consequence would have been to prevent the departure of the Government and of the two Chambers for North Africa, I must stress the point that I was supposed to have done all this not in the role of minister (as I was not a minister) but merely as a member of Parliament, and, being so, it is difficult to imagine how I could have exercised such power as a mere member of Parliament. The truth is that among those who might have left for North Africa there was a complete lack of will or wish to depart. Had it been otherwise it must seem that I had almost supernatural powers of persuasion, because clearly I had no authority whatever to prevent this departure, and no means to prevent the realisation of such a design. I must sincerely state that had I been in the place of the then ministers and had I wished to go to North Africa, I should never have allowed myself to be dissuaded by the opposition of a few members of Parliament, particularly when this opposition was merely verbal. Had I really been convinced of the utility of going to Africa, I should have used all my energy to persuade those members of Parliament who held a contrary view that the decision to leave for North Africa was a sound one. Had the opposition continued, I should have ignored it. (I cite in this connection the testimony of Paul Reynaud at Marshal Pétain's trial.)

At this point it would seem that an effort must be made to explain and justify the armistice. Clearly it is up to the Government which signed the armistice to justify this action in the first instance. I believe that the hearings at the Pétain trial have demonstrated without the shadow of a doubt that it was impossible to escape the sad necessity of taking this action. I do not attribute the importance which some persons are inclined to give it to the distinction between an order to cease fire and an armistice. In both cases the meaning in fact was that the army was in the hands of the enemy and France was left powerless. The only possible difference indeed is that under the first alternative the number of prisoners in the hands of the enemy would have been greater.

The truth, which certain witnesses in the Pétain trial seemed to have forgotten completely, is that the Commander-in-Chief could not at that moment even convey his orders to the army; the entire French Army was in a chaotic situation, separated in isolated groups, divided and retreating in disorder. General Weygand had pointed out that the invasion was moving with alarming rapidity and that we were losing, as prisoners, more and more of our men each day. The suggestion advanced to-day as an afterthought is that the army might have been directed towards the Britanny area to gain the protection of the British Fleet. This plan was impossible at the moment. Moreover, it must be remembered that the Germans had control of the air at that time and would have reduced very rapidly the forces grouped in the Breton peninsula. The only alternative solution was the continuation of the battle, with North Africa as a base.

And it is I, according to the charge brought against me, who am supposed to have prevented the transfer of the Seat of French sovereignty to North Africa. I shall comment on this as follows: I was not asked to take part in any parliamentary discussion upon the necessity or the opportunity of a departure of the Government for North Africa; I was not made conversant with any of the reasons which might have been advanced to justify this departure, and as a consequence I was never called upon to refute them. If it is true that the President of the Republic and the presidents of the Senate and Chamber, MM. Jeannenay and Herriot, believed that this course was necessary, why did they not make some effort, by propaganda and persuasion, even if they did not wish to go so far as convening formal sessions of parliamentary bodies, to convince those who, like myself, did not believe in the utility of such a course?

Had it been thought desirable to continue the fight from North Africa, preliminary steps should have been taken by the competent General Staffs. Arrangements should have been made for the transportation of the members of the Government and others. But we have the testimony of Admiral Darlan to the effect that this move was not practicable.

When I speak of transport I mean the transportation of troops and material, not merely of members of the Government and Parliament. This problem had to be judged in military terms. We all knew, even those who were not privileged to participate in the Government, that North Africa had no machinery for manufacturing war material, that no preparation whatsoever had been made for the reception of military forces in that area, that everything remained to be done or improvised. The other side of the picture was that, had the Government attempted to continue the fight from North Africa, the whole of France would immediately have been occupied.

In short, had there been the slightest chance of a favourable result for this enterprise I should have been in favour of it. But there was not the minutest possibility that it would succeed and that an effective resistance might have been opposed to the German attack. The German military advantage was overwhelming at that time. It is quite evident that Spain would not have opposed, and was not in a position to oppose, for many reasons, the passage of German troops across its territory. England, at that critical moment, was concerned exclusively with the defence of the British Isles, with the reorganisation, as soon and as rapidly as possible, of its shattered forces, and with the speeding up of its production in order that it might have the material means to oppose the German invasion which it so greatly feared. Soviet Russia was the ally of Germany, and the United States, in those days, was neutral.

This was a period of lightning warfare and, honestly, I do not believe that the rock of Gibraltar alone would have sufficed, when we consider the superiority of German aviation at that juncture, to delay for any considerable length of time the passage of the German Army across the Straits into North Africa. It is very easy to write beautiful plans long after the event, but I am firmly convinced that had we followed the course of resistance from North Africa the German aggressor would have completed the defeat of our armies on the Continent of Europe with the defeat of our forces in North Africa.

At this point, other important questions remain to be asked: What, in this case, would have become of the French Government? Would it have sought refuge in London? And what would have become of the great mass of the French people, the forty million French people who remained behind in France? Would they have been administered by the Germans, as were the Belgians, the Dutch, and the Poles? Here we come to the heart of the problem. In brief, would it have been in the greater interest of France to abandon it to disorder and to the cruel domination of the conqueror rather than to make the attempt which, in fact, was made to hold off the conqueror by negotiation, thus alleviating, to some extent at least, the load of suffering and hardship? At that time it was impossible to foresee how long the armistice would last but it was patently clear that what was true for a short armistice was even more true for an armistice which, in fact, lasted four long years.

At this point, moreover, another important question

should be asked: What would Africa have become in the hands of the Germans? Obviously it would have been an ideal base for operations against Egypt and the Suez Canal. Its possession by the Germans would have facilitated a junction with the Japanese Navy, possibly for naval warfare, and at the very least for the exchange of raw materials. Consider the frightful difficulties this situation would have caused for the British, who were anxious to get on with the war and save their Empire which was so severely threatened! It must not be forgotten, and this cannot be repeated too often, that in 1940 Germany and the Soviet Union were allies. A whole series of conclusions may be drawn from this fact; not the least is the possibility that the Russo-German alliance would have continued in view of the large field of endeavor which the possession of North Africa by the Germans would have opened up to German and Russian expansion in the Near East, in Africa, and in Asia.

Finally, and above all, if we are speaking in good faith, it must be recognised that America would have had to find a platform other than North Africa from which to launch her counter-attacks on the German armies.

I do not believe that it is an exaggeration to say that the decision of the French Government not to leave for North Africa was in itself a certain and important victory which contributed materially to the subsequent fuller victory of all the Allies.

This recapitulation of the facts, made in good faith and according to good sense, should suffice to answer this particular charge against me, but I must cite a further fact in conclusion: It was Marshal Pétain himself who took the original step to dissuade the French Government from leaving for North Africa. He said, before arriving in Bordeaux and while he was still in Tours, that those who might contemplate leaving at that juncture were deserting in the face of the enemy. This public statement of the Marshal was the determining factor in convincing many of those who otherwise might have considered leaving for North Africa that it was their solemn duty to remain on French soil. Pétain had at that time a high moral standing which, together with his military authority, made him the uncontested arbiter of the tragic situation in which we found ourselves.

There was another possible solution for those who did not wish to remain on their native French soil. It was entirely feasible for them to go to London, thus underlining their refusal to accept the armistice and their determination to continue the fight. De Gaulle did this. Other French leaders might have done the same thing, but some had to remain behind in 1940 for no other reason than to save North Africa from the German wave which was rolling to the south. It was vitally necessary to save this African bastion. Generals Giraud and de Gaulle found it intact two years later, with an army in control under Chiefs whom the Government, that was carrying on in the metropolitan area, had succeeded in liberating from German prisoner camps. It was essential that during the years 1940-1942 a Government should remain in France to defend French interests during the occupation period, and, in the event of a German victory or of a compromise peace, to lessen the risks and attenuate the dangers of total defeat.

Can it be objected that this was not in conformity with the dictates of honour?

Where is honour to be found in such a case?

Honour is here. Honour is there wheresoever and in whatsoever form the interests of our country can best be defended.

CHAPTER 5

VICHY—THE NATIONAL ASSEMBLY

ONLY by attempting to reconstruct the state of affairs prevailing in France in June and July 1940 can we understand to-day why the French Parliament, without being influenced in any way by bargaining, intrigue, threats, promises, or otherwise, decided on 10 July 1940 to confer upon Marshal Pétain exceptional executive authority. And it should be noted that in the last analysis Parliament in truth did not confer these powers on Marshal Pétain as the Accusation states in error. In fact, the Marshal received his authority from M. Albert Lebrun, then President of the Republic. The proceedings of the Pétain trial revealed clearly that M. Lebrun took this step on the specific advice of M. Paul Reynaud. The Government during that period had been invested with extraordinary powers by virtue of the emergency law of 1939, and it had the power to act without the advice and consent of the two Chambers.

We must not overlook the fact that we are back in June 1940 and that we are in the City of Bordeaux. On their way to this town most Parliamentarians had suffered vicissitudes of such proportions that they could estimate without outside influence the extent of the disaster which had overtaken our country. Our army in chaos, many units abandoned by their officers, isolated groups of soldiers wandering aimlessly over the countryside—with happily here and there, to counterbalance the tragic picture, individual acts of that highest heroism which has distinguished Frenchmen in all periods of our country's history; this, I repeat, was the tragic picture of rout displayed for all eyes to see. As for the civilian part of the population, great streams of men, women, and children were pouring into the south, machine-gunned on the way.

In these circumstances, I venture to say that very few of the Parliamentarians at Bordeaux believed we would recover rapidly from our extremely desperate state. Those who did believe it maintained a discreet silence. Throughout the country, as well as in Parliament, Frenchmen were pinning their last remaining hopes on Pétain, who loomed as the sole available saviour of our country. At the same time, with this there was a mounting wave of anger directed against those who had so glibly led us into the war which it was clear we had now lost. Let each of us examine his conscience carefully. If he is at all honest he will be unable to pretend that the situation was other than what I have just described, or that the mass of French people had any sentiments other than these. Without the shadow of a doubt there were isolated Frenchmen who did not despair. There was a small handful of men who, even then, had the courage to face what would turn out to be four years of ceaseless battle. It so happened that their vision and courage were justified. But at that critical moment there were few Frenchmen who shared their optimism or who had the courage to rally to their side.

There was another group which I cannot pass over in silence. These were the men who were in power, who were responsible for the major decisions at that time, who could not bring themselves to admit their failure and who had led us to this abyss of misery and despair.

The Parliament shared to some extent this responsibility. True, it voted some military credits, but the results of its parsimony were there for all eyes to see. They spelt catastrophe. Further, the Parliament had failed to insist upon one of the most fundamental rights guaranteed the French people under the constitution, I mean the right to pass on a declaration of war. Parliament should have questioned the Government on the number of our effectives, on our available war materials, on the condition of our alliances, on the risks involved, and on the possibilities remaining for a peaceful solution, before permitting the Government to plunge us into such an adventure. This it did not do and I recall the secret session of 2 September 1939, when I sought an airing of the situation behind closed doors. The Government turned down this request and denied Parliament its fundamental right of discussing the opportuneness of a declaration of war.

The fact that war was declared without the vote of Parliament was so flagrant a violation of the Constitution of 1875 that I do not hesitate to describe it as constituting a *coup d'état*.

It is my personal view that to have denied to the Communist Deputies their fundamental right to represent the voters who had elected them was likewise a major violation of our constitutional rights; they were not a majority, but they expressed the views of a large percentage of our population.

The Government which plunged the country into war without the material means, not merely of winning it, but even of waging it successfully, was guilty of a grievous fault; but it was a fault which must be shared by many of the Parliamentarians of that time, who were either too weak or too listless to protest. I quote my statement of 9 November 1943, when I received the mayors of the Cantal district, among whom were many members of Parliament. Speaking of the Senate session of 2 September 1939, I said: *

'What was my object in requesting a secret session of the Senate? I might answer this by asking, What does the constitution provide? The constitution contains a sound provision. This is that France cannot and must not go to war without a vote of Parliament. Was a vote of Parliament requested or permitted? No, neither the Senate nor the Chamber were requested or permitted by the Government in power to vote for or against war. You who are republicans and to whom legal procedure means something must never forget that there was no legal basis for our entry into this war.'

* The full text of this heretofore unpublished address will be found in Appendix IV.

At Bordeaux, to continue, it was clear to an enormous majority of the senators and deputies that Hitler would be pitiless in his dealings with France if he were made to deal with certain French politicians. Everyone present on the scene at that time had but a single purpose: to save what could be saved and to reduce to a minimum the consequences of our disaster. Pétain's name was on every lip. The decision of Parliament to confer on the Marshal all necessary powers for a sufficient period to permit the country's recovery was an honourable one. There was a patriotic motive for this decision to reform those institutions which had brought us to the brink of disaster. Other than Pétain, there was nobody who could undertake the providential mission which all felt he alone was equipped to undertake. I merely shared this view with many others. If I was more active than some in seeking to implement this viewpoint it was because of my habit of working for the realisation of an object when I am convinced that it is a just one; above all, when I am convinced that it is in our country's best interest. It was not in the least necessary for me 'to intrigue, to promise, or to threaten'; my interlocutors required very little convincing.

Possibly I had some influence at that time with my audience; perhaps a little more than had certain others whom I can think of. I had made despairing appeals for peace in the Senate. I had predicted that unless France could forge a chain around Germany she would suffer disaster. Events, alas, had proved me right.

Once again I had become a member of the Cabinet and the Marshal had directed me to take upon myself the solution of this important question, just as, a few days later, he instructed me to be his representative in any discussions which might have to take place with the Germans. I was, in a word, his personal representative before Parliament. This he formally confirmed to the parliamentary delegation of war veterans which visited him on 6 July 1940 to discuss the plan about to be submitted to the National Assembly. MM. Jacquié, Chaumié, Paul Boncour, and Taurines on that same day drew up a report of their conversation with the Marshal. The following sentences are taken from their report: 'Coming to the specific purpose of our visit, he informed us that he had instructed President Laval to be his spokesman before Parliament and to treat with the individual members of Parliament regarding his proposal. The Marshal did not wish to participate personally in the debate.'

Thus it is evident that I was given the mission to discuss and defend the Government proposal before the two Houses separately and the National Assembly, and this I did by virtue of a specific mandate given me by the Marshal. There is a letter from him to this effect (now held under seal) which confirms the Marshal's explanation to the group of parliamentary war veterans. In other words, such activity as I deployed was not in a personal capacity but in execution of a specific mandate with which I was entrusted by the Government and by its head, Marshal Pétain.

What was involved was the necessity, under the law of 1875, of securing a favourable vote in each of the two Chambers before the National Assembly could be called and the Government's Bill laid before it.

It is interesting to note the reception accorded the Government's project by the senators and deputies voting separately on 9 July 1940. This will be a test of the accuracy of certain testimony introduced in the Pétain trial: the Chamber and Senate were asked to pass upon a Bill signed jointly 'Philippe Pétain' and 'Albert Lebrun,' as follows:

'The following draft resolution will be submitted to the Chamber of Deputies by the Marshal of France, President of the Council of Ministers, who is prepared to defend it in debate.

'The Chamber of Deputies declares that the constitutional laws should be reformed.'

The identical text was presented to the Senate this very same day.

In the Chamber it was upheld by 395 votes to three (MM. Roche, Biondi, and Margaine).

In the Senate there was only one opposing vote, that of the Marquis de Chambrun.

During the two debates there was no real opposition to the Government's Bill.

M. Jeanneney, President of the Senate, spoke these words in the course of his statement:

'I bear witness to our veneration for Marshal Pétain and our heartfelt gratitude for this new gift of his person to his country.'

M. Harriot, President of the Chamber, used similar terms in his address.

The following morning, 10 July, a secret session of the National Assembly was held in order that the Government's measure might be discussed freely before it was submitted to the afternoon session at a formal sitting. An official short-hand report was made of this meeting, which can be found in the National Archives. Here is the text of the Government's proposed measure as it was presented to the National Assembly:

'The National Assembly gives full powers to the Government of the Republic under the signature and authority of Marshal Pétain, President of the Council, to promulgate in one or several measures the new constitution of the French State. This constitution shall guarantee the rights of labour, of the family, and of the Fatherland. It shall be ratified by the nation and applied by the Assembly which it brings into being.'

It is the fashion to-day to suggest that the vote on this constitutional law was falsified. Does anybody really take this allegation seriously? Every member of Parliament had at least three opportunities to make his position clear, or to reconsider it, during the session of 9 July or during one of the sessions of 10 July.

Moreover, there was the counter-proposal of the war veterans, which gave rise to an extensive debate and even to a modification of the text of the Government proposal in the sense that the provision for ratification was amended. The war veterans won their point. The measure was finally drafted as given above and presented to the National Assembly.

In the secret session there was every opportunity for discussion. No protest was registered; no revision was sought. It is curious indeed that we have had to wait four years for the charge to be made that the vote was falsified. This view would have carried greater weight had it been uttered at the time. (The measure was approved by 569 votes to eighty, with seventeen abstentions.)

In this connection I was greatly surprised to read certain portions of the testimony at the Pétain trial. Some witnesses were apparently more than ready to talk in August 1945 who maintained a discreet silence at Bordeaux, and, subsequently, at Vichy. Truth is that the expression of their viewpoint might have been of greater service to the country in June and July 1940, when it might have influenced or modified decisions against which these very persons now tardily and impotently inveigh. I have no idea on what backstairs gossip the charge is based that I manœuvred and intrigued, promised, and threatened to get the constitutional law through the Assembly. Doubtless it is useful for some to-day, and, of course, it is not very difficult, four years after the event, to find some pretext to justify one's vote; I shall merely observe that had some minister other than myself presented the Government Bill the vote would have been precisely the same. Perhaps the wisest and most objective course will be to discuss M. Léon Blum's testimony at the Marshal's trial. He asserted that the law of 10 July was voted under the triple threat of Doriot's gang at Vichy, Weygand at Clermont-Ferrand, and of the Germans at Moulins. I was not aware that Doriot's gangsters were active at Vichy in those days. It is true the Germans were at Moulins, but at that time neither I nor anyone else knew what they intended to do. My first contact with them took place ten days later in Paris, on 20 July to be precise. I cannot imagine, therefore, how or to what extent they concerned themselves with the debate in the National Assembly. I had heard a rumour of a possible French army '*putsch*' and I suppose this is what M. Léon Blum means when he speaks of 'Weygand at Clermont.' Personally, I did not take this rumour seriously although I must admit that many members of Parliament seemed to be impressed by it. By this I do not mean to suggest that I was in agreement with General Weygand. He showed towards me, whenever a contact between us was necessary, the same disregard which he showed for all republican parliamentarians.

During the Pétain trial the atmosphere at Vichy on that fateful day of 10 July was painted in sombre colours. I was not Minister of the Interior at the time and, therefore, may not, as a consequence, have been thoroughly informed on what was taking place. But in all honesty I do not recall an atmosphere in any sense as dark as is now painted. I need hardly add that Doriot's gangsters honoured me only by regarding me as one of their principal enemies. This they proved time and again during the four years of the German occupation and more than once their threats against my life were quite specific.

In actual fact, the political climate of that day was the consequence of defeat, of the tragic exodus of the population along the machine-gunned roads of France, of the Calvary of hundreds of thousands of men, women, and children yearning to return to their homes. They could not return because France was divided into two zones by a demarcation line which could not be crossed. But to revert to the constitutional question, there was one point with regard to which Parliament was virtually unanimous: this was the necessity of constitutional reform. My role was that of a minister mandated by the head of the Government to defend the Government's proposal before Parliament. The fact that I succeeded—and anybody else would have succeeded had he been in my place—does not in any sense mean that I had to manœuvre or to intrigue. In order to justify this thesis it must be supposed that there was a majority in opposition to this proposal; in fact, the majority loudly demanded it, or it must be imagined that I had extraordinary powers of suggestion over the two Chambers. This, to say the least, would not have been very complimentary to those who should have crossed swords with me but who, in fact, remained stonily silent.

I could also show that the war veterans association's counter-proposal was more drastic than the Government proposal. Had I had the slightest intention of staging a *coup d'état* I should have adopted their counter-proposal, which provided for the suspension of the constitution of 1875 until peace was concluded, which did not provide for a Government of the Republic, but solely for the personal rule of Marshal Pétain, and which called for a new constitution.

These facts cited above must be taken as conclusive evidence that it was not necessary for me to threaten or make any promises to bring about a favourable vote in the National Assembly and that I did not have to resort to any special pressure to secure the adoption of a measure which was ardently desired by an overwhelming majority of our country's representatives. The two Chambers were legally called together and so was the National Assembly. The debates followed the normal procedure and the vote which culminated the sessions was not, and could not, have been tarnished by any possible irregularity.

CHAPTER 6

AFTER THE VOTE OF 10 JULY 1940

MY DIFFERENCES WITH
MARSHAL PÉTAIN

WHEN I testified at Marshal Pétain's trial I made it indisputably clear that I was at no time in agreement with his domestic policies. Nevertheless, charges are levelled against me concerning activities for which the Marshal was solely responsible, or perhaps I should say the Marshal and the little group of his personal counsellors of whose activities I never approved.

The Marshal made a fundamental mistake at the outset, which he repeated regularly thereafter: he refused to subject his decisions to the approval of the Council of Ministers.

On the morrow of the vote and after he had signed the first constitutional measure in the style 'We, Philippe Pétain', I realised the mistake which I had made and I shared the fears of those in and out of Parliament who had not envisaged the personal stamp with which the Marshal was to impress his rule.

Then there was the Act, which he signed, providing that I should succeed to his office in the event that he was obliged, for one reason or another, to vacate it. This was in strict accordance with the understanding of those who, in the National Assembly, voted the Government's measure and who could not ignore the possibility that the Marshal might not survive the critical situation in which the country found itself. There can be no doubt that had my name been inserted in the Government's Bill under that of the Marshal the Bill would have been voted with the same majority.

The members of Parliament, as M. Léon Blum emphasised, feared an army coup to the detriment of the civil authority, and this alone would have assured a majority for a text including my name. And I might add that there was no criticism at that time by any of those who voted the Marshal's decree in the National Assembly.

Had the Marshal for some reason been prevented from continuing actively in office and had I, under these circumstances, been obliged to assume the executive authority, I should have had a conception of my role very different from his. Despite the extraordinary power which had been delegated, and this had been necessitated by the enemy occupation, I should have turned to Parliament. Indeed, I am aware of no other direction in which I might have turned for essential support.

I wish to record with great emphasis that I should never have accepted succession to the Marshal's office unless I had been assured of the active collaboration of Parliament, and unless the representatives of Parliament best qualified had agreed to share with me the responsibility of office pending the return of normal conditions.

Again, had I really placed any value on the Marshal's decree naming me as his successor, I might, when I returned to office in 1942, have requested another decree again naming me the Marshal's successor and cancelling the decision of 13 December 1940. I did not request this renewal for the very good reason that circumstances had altered radically and little resembled the situation following the Assembly's vote on 10 July 1940.

There was, moreover, another good reason why I did not wish to be named the Marshal's successor and this was that the Marshal decreed that after Darlan's death I should remain in power only one month and that, after that, the Council of Ministers should designate a successor and determinate the relationship of the Chief of State and the head of the Government. For my part, I believed it necessary to have both a President of the Republic and a head of the Government or Prime Minister.

It should be noted, furthermore, that the Marshal was

mandated by Parliament to promulgate a new constitution. He never fulfilled this mandate. Time and again I reminded him of his duty in this respect. Invariably he replied with some vague formula. Our fundamental disagreement on the fundamental constitutional question prevented him from discussing with me his constitutional project.

He had innumerable personal collaborators. Some were temporary, others permanent, as for example, Admiral Fernet. These collaborators prepared and accumulated projects which never saw the light of day, if we except the message which the Marshal proposed to read over the radio on 13 November 1943, announcing that he had drafted a new constitution. The Germans forbade that broadcast. This was the draft constitution which was produced during the Marshal's trial. It provided for a return to the Republic, but only after his death, because the Marshal could not admit that he could be replaced during his lifetime. As head of the Government I had no knowledge of this project but I was informed by a colonel who was a close collaborator of the Marshal that it envisaged the return to office of M. Camille Chautemps.

When I expressed the Government's views during the close of the session of the National Assembly on 10 July 1940, I emphasised very clearly that the new constitution must not be reactionary in tone, that it must not be haunted by the spirit of a vanished past and that it must echo the wishes of the French people. I added, moreover, that any constitution which failed to embody the precise wishes of the people would be artificial and would not be ratified. The language which I used before the Assembly was so clear and specific as to leave no doubt regarding the republican character of the proposed reform.

Before the special committee which had the responsibility of reporting the proposed law for constitutional reform I solemnly pledged that the presidents of the committees on universal suffrage of the Chamber and of the committee on civil legislation of the Senate would participate in the drafting of the new constitution. Moreover, I stressed that their very presence would serve as a guarantee that the new constitution would be inspired by our republican antecedents and the spirit of the laws of the Republic. The Chamber would have the budgetary control over public expenditures.

Nothing can be found in the records of the proceedings leading to the adoption of the law of 10 July 1940 which could possibly justify a suggestion that I wished or sought to violate or to vitiate the principles of republican legality. Indeed, the Accusation has to go far afield to find a statement, which I am supposed to have made to a group of schoolteachers at Mayet de Montagne a few years later, in order to assert that on 10 July 1940 I had taken the first step in a 'National Revolution'.

To this absurd allegation I shall oppose the words I uttered on 10 July 1940, and which cannot be contradicted because they were spoken before the National Assembly and were recorded at the time. To-day they possess an official and historical character. Here is what I said:

'No brutality, no regime of force can crush the pride of our race. If we remain strong and resolute, if we are determined to fortify our souls, then there may spring from the great tragedy that was our defeat a final gain for our country.

'When a constitution is framed it is not conceivable even to suggest that it should not be the expression of the customs, the wishes, the aspirations, and the will of the country. Failing this, any attempt would be vain and artificial and would be swept away by events. It is not a task of this type that we are undertaking.

'The constitution we have in mind cannot be reactionary and in France's present condition we cannot look backwards nor revert to the past. It is forwards, towards the future, that we must look. We must give to the working classes, not only the guarantee of free elections, but rights, real rights, under an impartial control by the State.

'There is another thing we have in mind: we are concerned with our moral heritage. We have in mind the family, the rights inherent in every human being and which constitute our reason for living.'

I might continue to list excerpts of this kind but the above should suffice. My words are clear enough to obviate any risk of misinterpretation. I never bowed before Nazism or Fascism when I stated: 'No brutality, no regime of force can crush the pride of our race,' or when I said: 'We do not wish to impose upon France a constitution which would not be the expression of her will,' adding that 'such an attempt would be vain and artificial and would be swept away by events'.

I did not envisage a reactionary constitution. My language could not have been clearer when I took the position that it was impossible to 'revert to the past'.

Can one march more directly towards a republican regime or more clearly condemn a dictatorship? There was no room for any more doubt after I stated: 'We are concerned with our moral heritage. We have in mind the family, the rights inherent in every human being and which constitute our reason for living.'

On 5 June 1943, speaking of the future peace in a message broadcast at a time when our country was entirely occupied by the enemy, I went so far as to say:

'The individual character of each people must be respected. No country can impose its customs, its religion and its regime upon others. Nevertheless, all political regimes must have one common aspect: they must be based upon the will of the people. Labour must have everywhere that leading place which is due it and without which any political institution will fail because the support of the masses will be lacking.'

How is it possible, in these statements, to discover a desire to imitate the German regime? Is it not rather the same language which has often been employed since the liberation, and were not these sentences prophetic at the time they were uttered?

How can one deny upon re-reading them that they constitute the doctrine of a free republic and, as I expressed it at the time, of 'a new, stronger, more humane republic'.

How can one fail to see my condemnation of the Marshal's reactionary internal policy in these words: 'those who, in my country, dream of the possibility of a return to the past are mistaken. France does not wish it. France will not consent to going backwards'.

I recall having spoken at Mayet de Montagne to a group of Marshal Pétain's professional propagandists. For the most part they came from the extreme Right and could not, therefore, be supposed to have any regard or affection for me. I recall having talked with them informally and having reviewed for them in a conversational tone the high points of French foreign policy before the war. I do not remember referring to the constitutional problem. I probably spoke ironically to them (as I did to many others on many occasions) about 'the Marshal's National Revolution' as the patent medicine expected to cure every ill, according to these men's ideals, their dreams, and their ambitions. I spoke thus to the legionaries. I used this metaphor when I addressed the mayors and prefects. Moreover, it was generally known that I was the uncompromising adversary of this reactionary concept.

Throughout the occupation I never missed an opportunity in my radio broadcasts to speak of the Republic, all the more so because I had to remind the Marshal, his personal collaborators, the band of adventurers and the royalists, that the country would accept no regime other than that of the Republic.

The German-controlled Paris newspapers never failed to attack me for using these terms and the collaborationist parties snapped at me with uncontrolled ferocity on this score. For the so-called 'collaborationist' newspapers of Paris I was the 'Republican strong man'. This was because I

Pierre Laval and Stalin in Moscow, 1935

Pierre Laval with the present Pope, Pius XII, at the Vatican in 1935

Pierre Laval with Mr. and Mrs. Henry L. Stimson in Washington, 1931

had stated to the United Press in May 1941: 'We will build a new, a stronger, and a more humane republic.' I added on that occasion: 'Will our liberties survive? There can be no question of their disappearance in a country which was their birthplace,' and in September 1942 I stated: 'We can only construct a free republic when we ourselves are wholly free.'

The suppression of the office of the President of the Republic and the full powers which the Marshal assumed were the result of constitutional measures in which I had no part. Their authors were M. Alibert, who was political adviser to the Marshal, and probably other advisers. I was at no time consulted regarding these measures. I realised at once what abuse of power these measures represented, but I was sure that they would have only an ephemeral existence. Nobody thought at that early date that the Armistice would last four long years.

In all truth I was systematically ignored whenever discussions took place with regard to the internal political aims of the Government: the very fact that I was a parliamentarian rendered me suspect. Thus it was like a bolt from the blue when I learned one day from General Weygand, at a meeting of the Council of Ministers, that the Legion of War Veterans had been founded and all other groups dissolved. The new group, I was told, would be the only officially recognised political association and would stem straight from the Marshal. This was the group which, in turn, ultimately gave birth to the Militia.

Thenceforth, the Prefects and even the ministers had to take into account the 'Legion'. Its activities were not always commendable. I stated on several occasions that the Legion was the revenge of those who had lost in the pre-war elections. At all events, it was destined to play a decisive role in the internal evolution of the State.

In sum, it is unjust to hold me responsible for acts with which I had absolutely nothing to do and which, moreover, I thoroughly disapproved. The summoning, the meeting, and the voting of the National Assembly in July 1940 were wholly legal. No charge can be levelled against me on this ground. I could not, had I wanted to, influence 700 members of Parliament. Nobody thought fit to protest at that time, not even those who were surprised by the heavy majority vote.

As regards the abuses which were committed in the application of the law of constitutional reform I repeat that I had no part in any of this. I stress again that the Marshal was too jealous of his authority to allow me to trespass on a preserve which he regarded as exclusively his own. As a parliamentarian I was too suspect for him to ask my advice.

Often I protested that to substitute one municipal officer for another, particularly when the dismissed official had been regularly elected, was an arbitrary action which was bound to have unfortunate repercussions. I was especially concerned about this because my political friends were very often the victims of this short-sighted policy, both in the Puy de Dôme and in the Seine. Moreover, these shifts were often made with a total disregard of the sentiments of the local population. It was sheer folly to revoke a man like Bétoulle, who for so many years had been Mayor of Limoges.

I was even more opposed to the Marshal's policy of changing the municipal councils, particularly as this was irreconciliable with the stand which I had taken before the National Assembly. It was the Legion which was authorised to make these changes in the Southern Zone. The Prefects and the Minister of the Interior were allowed merely to ratify what had already been accomplished by the Legion.

Here I must note that the general councils were suppressed in 1941 when I was not a member of the Government. This was a flagrant violation of the spirit in which the law of July 1940 had been voted.

Furthermore, a National Council, all the members of which were designated by the Marshal, was created while I was out of office. I dissolved this body immediately upon my return.

I strove to re-establish progressively the pre-war general

councils. The only change was in the new name of 'departmental councils'; the rights and duties of these bodies remained the same. On many occasions I was obliged to bow to the will of the Legion in appointing the members, but I sought as much as possible to appoint councillors who had been elected before the war, and I instructed the Prefects to propose the names of elected councillors whenever feasible. This was the device which I hit upon to restore after 1942 these elective bodies, which in 1940 and 1941 the Marshal had suppressed.

I was in no way responsible for the personal power seized by the Marshal. Those who know what my relations with the Marshal were, and who experienced the atmosphere of Vichy, will be the first to recognise that his policy, in this respect, was not mine, and that often it was aimed against me. I had nothing to do, for instance, with the substitution of the term 'French State' for 'French Republic' in official documents. The removal of the statuettes of the Republic, the new-style oath, which I always refused to take, the effigy on the postage stamps, all the thousand and one ludicrous, and at the same time illegal, measures originated with those who wished to strengthen the personal power of the Marshal. At my offices, both in Paris and in Vichy, however, I never failed to use the letter-head of the French Republic.

Another time, I discovered that the Marshal, in the course of a luncheon, had suggested to the Keeper of the Seals that the title 'Public Prosecutor of the Republic' should be changed to 'State Prosecutor'. I rebuked the Keeper of the Seals because he had failed to tell me this. Had I known this, I should have gone immediately to the Marshal to protest. In any event, the Keeper of the Seals did not make the change, on the pretext that he would have had to modify too many articles of the Code. Here again I should purely and simply have refused, stressing that this was a violation of the constitutional law.

During the Pétain trial a juryman asked me whether I had promised to continue the parliamentary remuneration.

I do not recall that this question was raised but, in any event, there is no doubt but that in agreement with the Government the members of Parliament received a retirement fee. Their remuneration was perhaps reduced because of the fact that they did not acquiesce in acceptance of the principle of retirement, and in my own personal case I consistently refused to draw my remuneration in that form; believing that it implied an acceptance of the suppression of the Chambers. This small fact is the best evidence of my state of mind regarding Parliament and its legal continuity.

Finally, the Act of Accusation states that this absolutist form of government could have been established only with 'the support of the invader and copying his methods'.

It would be more correct to state that the law of 10 July 1940 was one of the consequences of our defeat and one of the devices conceived to defend as best we could the interests of our country. It would be completely false and entirely unjust to suggest that I was the sponsor of that personal power for the Marshal, which the Act of Accusation describes as 'absolutism'. Contrary to what the Accusation implies, not long after 10 July (on 13 December 1940, to be exact) I myself was the victim of this abuse of power. I have mentioned previously that the decree naming me heir apparent to the Marshal was in accordance with the terms of the Assembly debate. Happily, it was never necessary to give effect to this provision and, had it been necessary, as I have already asserted, I should have looked for support from Parliament. In any event it was a very ephemeral privilege since it was cancelled on 13 December 1940, and was doubtless the basis for my arrest, the main purpose of which was to satisfy the personal ambition of Admiral Darlan. As I have stated before, I might, had I wished it, have reassumed the title of successor when I returned to power on 18 April 1942. I did not seek and would not have accepted this title, which shows that I had no personal desire to inherit the Marshal's responsibility. In fairness to Admiral Darlan I should place on record here my belief that, as one who was accustomed to move in parliamentary and ministerial circles and as the son of a minister, he was a loyal Republican, and I have no reason to doubt his loyalty to the Republican Constitution and his intention of returning to its normal operation when the occupation ended. As spokesman for the Marshal before the National Assembly I had shouldered a grave responsibility *vis à vis* my colleagues: I was to some extent the guarantor of the agreements into which I had been obliged to enter. In giving these pledges I had guaranteed the Marshal's intention of carrying them out and so had my colleagues who voted for them.

I could not foresee, nor could anyone else imagine, that immediately following the vote, the Marshal would give, or would allow to be given in his name, a distinctly personal character to his rule.

There is no need for me to observe here that I was not consulted in the choice of his ministers, and naturally it follows that I had no part at all in the selection of his immediate collaborators. It was clear to me from the beginning that the Marshal was not a bit interested in republican legality. I concluded this from the pretentious and obsolete style in which he signed his first decree: 'We, Philippe Pétain', even more than from the provision of the decree itself, which I regarded as nebulous. Like everyone else I believed that the German occupation would last only a relatively short time.

An incredible propaganda was organised and an extraordinary advertising campaign was launched throughout the country. Photographs and busts of Pétain were everywhere. The newspapers, the radio, the cinema, spoke of him constantly. His smallest gestures took the lead over all other news in the chronicles of the time.

There was the national song: 'Marshal, here we are.' There was a new decoration: the Marshal's order, bearing a battle-axe. Groups were organized to spread the Marshal's gospel—the 'Friends of the Marshal', in the Occupied Zone; and the Legion, in the Free Zone. I am certain that there is no precedent in French history for so much propaganda about one man.

My relations with the Marshal were correct and courteous, but never intimate; and after the voting in the National Assembly he never admitted me into his private councils regarding domestic politics. Far from being his adviser, when I proffered an opinion the opposite course was almost always followed.

I must insist, therefore, that I cannot be blamed for the Marshal's reactionary measures. Almost invariably they were taken behind my back, against my will, and very often in the face of my specific opposition. The Marshal, then, was the supreme head of the State, and he was scornful of the normal practices of government, of which he was completely ignorant; just as ignorant, in fact, as were his new ministers. He worked privately and the most important measures reached the Council of Ministers solely for their information.

Moreover, as I was a minister without portfolio I did not participate in the drafting of the texts and this applied to measures of such importance as setting up the professional committees, the formulation of the labour code, and the measures directed against the Jews and secret societies. The Marshal was jealous of his prerogatives and no shadow of opposition was tolerated by him. Such was the political situation immediately following 10 July 1940.

Perhaps all these remarks will help to clarify the reason why I, who was responsible for piloting the Government's Bill through the National Assembly, did not reject off-hand the position of 'heir apparent'. It would have permitted me to hold office, in the event that the Marshal could not have continued at his post, and to restore a normal and legal conduct of government. As it happened, this title brought down on my head the hostility of many whose ambitions it seemed to thwart and I strongly believe that it was the underlying cause of my eviction from office and my arrest on 13 December 1940.

The step taken against me that day is sufficient evidence of the extremely limited scope of my authority which impressed the other ministers very little.

As regards the purpose which is to-day imputed to me by my accusers, I should have been quite out of my mind to entertain any such ambition. I had too much political experience to believe that France, upon regaining her liberty, would tolerate for long a regime based on police power and on force. In order to be a successful dictator a man must curry popular favour, and this I have never sought. The tasks which I have performed in times of crisis when other political leaders refused to serve have been in the line of duty to my country but have never enhanced my popularity, something indispensable to a man with dictatorial ambitions.

Even the most casual examination of my political career will prove conclusively that never having sought popularity I never aspired to be a dictator.

The German occupation obliged our Government to take a number of measures such as those regarding the Jews and Freemasons. I was not the author of these measures and I will show that, in fact, my whole effort was to nullify them. Of course, I might then have run away and abandoned our country to certain adventurers or to the tender mercy of the conqueror. Had I the right to do this? Later, I shall prove that I did not have this right.

And it is within this framework that the answer to the whole problem must be found.

CHAPTER 7

22 OCTOBER 1940: MONTOIRE

WHY should I have committed treason? For money? That would have been the most unspeakable crime. My accusers do not suggest it.

Was it to satisfy my vanity or to fulfil an ambition? I have occupied eighteen ministerial posts and I was several times Prime Minister. I had the proud responsibility of representing our country and of speaking in its name when it was strong and victorious. When I, who had no responsibility for the declaration of war, for the course of the war, nor for the defeat, agreed to speak for France when she was beaten and weak and unhappy, it was to defend my country, not to betray it.

Let us consider the facts:

In July 1940, before the meeting of the National Assembly, I received a call at Vichy from a newspaper-man, a certain Fontenoy. He informed me of the desire of Herr Abetz, the German Ambassador in Paris, to meet me and discuss certain problems then pending. I informed the Marshal of this call and it was following my report to the Marshal that I was requested by him, about 20 July, to establish a liaison with the German Embassy, and I proceeded to Paris.

My first meeting with Herr Abetz was cold and distant, but correct. I had never met him before and he naturally remained on the defensive.

The Armistice Convention was so brutal that, had it been strictly applied according to the written word and in the spirit of the established text, our country would not have been able to live. I conceived my role as that of a special spokesman for my country; by speech, negotiation, and action I attempted to pry loose Germany's stranglehold. As a secondary role, I felt that I must obtain for France the most favourable terms when the peace came to be signed.

At this time, when the chances of a German victory appeared very good, I was determined that France should not lose a square inch of her home territory nor yet of her colonial Empire. This I had the courage to state publicly several times during enemy occupation. I had *Mein Kampf* well in mind and knew that we could expect almost anything from Hitler's ambition. At that particular moment the conquerors maintained, under orders of course, a correct attitude, and they appeared to wish to spare the French people useless humiliation.

During this preliminary period the Germans with whom I came into contact said nothing to which I could take offence, if I except General Medicus who reminded me that we had been beaten. I replied at once that were it otherwise I should not be speaking to him.

Incidentally, it was at about this time that Abetz hinted to me that the peace treaty, when it was offered, would be a harsh one. He made this remark on the way to Fontainebleau where I was to have a meeting with Marshal von Brauchitsch, and added, 'It seems unjust that you should be making this visit to a German Marshal in a French city'.

Ambassador Abetz reminded me that for many years he had attempted to bring about a rapprochement between our two countries. 'My views have not changed,' he said, 'but there are powerful German personalities who think otherwise.' I asked him to help me in obtaining for France at least some lightening of her burden. First of all, I sought the liberation of our prisoners, the elimination of the demarcation line in the North and around the Pas-de-Calais, and a diminution of the occupation costs. He promised to help me and to pave the way for a meeting with his Minister, von Ribbentrop, which would permit me to renew my requests on a higher plane. Several weeks later, about 20 October, I was informed by Abetz that von Ribbentrop had arrived in France and that I would see him. He enjoined me to keep the meeting absolutely secret and I agreed to this except that I informed him I must tell the Marshal, and this I did at once.

On Tuesday morning, 22 October, I left Paris in the company of Abetz. We took the direction of Rambouillet. Abetz, however, refused to tell me exactly where the meeting would take place, pretending that he himself was not informed. 'We are going first to Tours and from there we shall be directed to von Ribbentrop.' We continued our journey and it was only that evening, at about 6.30, after having left Tours, that the Ambassador revealed to me that it was Hitler whom I was to meet and that von Ribbentrop would be present also. It was on receiving this information that the words escaped me: *'Sans blague!'* which have been quoted in the world Press.

It is therefore clear as day that I did not, as accused, engineer this meeting. I take my oath that the true facts are exactly as I have stated them.

Was a meeting with Hitler at that time a mistake?

Was it possible to avoid this meeting?

When it is understood that my mission was to defend France's interests against the Germans the conclusion must be accepted that it was quite natural and desirable that I should meet the German leader for this purpose.

If we start from the assumption that the Armistice was a mistake (a crime, according to the State Prosecutor), then it is understandable that I should be criticised for taking part in this meeting. But, as I have stated many times before, I did not sign the Armistice nor did I have any part in approving it.

When I came on the scene, the Armistice was already an accomplished fact and the Wehrmacht occupied our country. From 1914 to 1918 a section of our country had been in its grip, and as I travelled to Montoire I had in mind the ravages of which the Germans had then been guilty, on this previous occasion, in our Northern and our Eastern departments.

Possibly those in Washington and London who have since

criticised my policy had forgotten this tragic period of our country's history, when the population of the conquered provinces was deported *en masse* after the conqueror had stolen all furniture, goods, even the grain and the cattle from the fields. If such had been the German attitude in 1914, during a war declared by Germany against France, what would be their attitude in 1940 in a war which France herself had declared against Germany and in which the German armies had been wholly victorious?

Consider for a minute and you will agree that any honest Frenchman placed in the position which I occupied in 1940 would have done anything to prevent a repetition of the German ravages of 1914-1918. During that war they had been confined to several departments only; this time they were to be spread over the whole of France.

I had accepted the difficult role of defending our interests and had agreed to maintain contact with the German Government. How better could I carry out my mission than by speaking with Hitler? And, to be absolutely frank, how could I have escaped, under the circumstances in which I found myself, a meeting which had not been prepared by me and with regard to which I had had no advance notice?

I testified during the Pétain trial about the circumstances of the invitation to the Marshal and I stated that he made no objection to proceeding to Montoire two days later, that is on Thursday, 24 October.

After a preliminary conversation with me, Hitler went to Hendaye for a meeting with Franco, and I learned some time later from Abetz that during this meeting Hitler turned down Franco's demands for a part of French Morocco. I claim in all modesty that this result, favourable to my country, was due at least in part to my preliminary conversation with Hitler.

If Montoire is placed in its true frame, if the facts and data are recalled, it must be admitted that this meeting with its attendant circumstances was normal and natural. Of course, if the fiction is upheld that the Armistice was not

necessary and that we should have continued the battle from
North Africa, it might be otherwise, but in that event the
mistake is not Montoire, the 'crime' is the Armistice. I have
already stated that I entered the Government after the
Armistice, and whatever my personal opinion of the Armistice may have been with regard to its necessity, this opinion
did not and could not have influenced the decision that was
taken at the time. It is very easy afterwards to claim all sorts
of wisdom and foresight, but the cruel fact was that at that
time we were beaten and that, with the remnants of our fleet
and the few men and the small amount of material which we
still possessed, a military recovery was out of the question.

It is an easy thing, five years afterwards, to refight the war
and to disprove the arguments used at that time. But it is
a grave injustice to accuse of 'intelligence with the enemy'
those who, like myself, sought to defend our country and who
had no means of doing so save day-by-day negotiation.

In a word, Montoire was not the result of intrigue but the
logical consequence of events. The 1918 Armistice had been
concluded for a period of thirty-six days; the 1940 Armistice
had no time limit and was supposed to remain in effect until
a treaty of peace was signed. It is true that a great many
persons believed in an early defeat of England, and as a
consequence in a short armistice.

The French plenipotentiaries had been directed by the
Government to ascertain what would be the peace terms
offered by Germany, but their request remained unanswered.

The terms of this Armistice without time limit were
harsh. The whole economic life of France was subordinated
to the whims of the German Military Commission.

What could be more normal, what more vitally necessary
for the French Government than to seize an occasion like
Montoire in order at least to learn what were Germany's
immediate and future intentions towards our country? Even
had the Montoire meeting had no other purpose, this would
justify it. There is no reason to seek a criminal purpose

when the only object of the meeting on our side was to defend the interests of France.

To call the Montoire conversation 'intelligence with the enemy' and 'treason' is a desecration of the truth.

Up to the present time no judge has questioned me about Montoire nor has the slightest curiosity been manifested in this regard. Yet it would seem to be a natural subject for questioning.

I kept careful notes of the meeting of 22 October when I was alone on the French side and also of that of 24 October when I accompanied the Marshal. These notes are in my dossier under seal.

During these two conversations Hitler declared that he had offered peace to France and that France's reply had been to declare war on Germany without any solid reason. He said that he did not wish Germany to meet the cost of the war, then mounting considerably.

France could, if she wished, await the end of hostilities and hope for the exhaustion of Germany, but he warned me that 'if England should offer a compromise peace I will not add to Germany's sufferings by sparing France'.

He used the word 'collaboration' but did not define what he meant. He said that he was absolutely sure of final victory in a very brief period and he listed the means at his disposal in men and matériel, and particularly underscored Germany's war potential in armament factories.

He spoke, too, at length, about Africa. As he had dwelt on the German blood which had been shed in Europe, I responded that Africa was for us sacred ground because it had been watered with French blood. At this point he hinted at the possibility of economic collaboration, but he gave no exact details.

'You can crush us because you are the stronger,' I told Hitler; 'we shall suffer, we shall endure, and because it is a natural law, one day we shall rise in revolt. You have beaten us, yes; but in the past we have beaten you. It is your purpose to humiliate us; at a date and under circumstances which cannot yet be determined, the bloody drama between our two countries will be renewed. Our flags have seen enough victories. If you offer us a just peace which takes into account our honour and our interests, anything may be possible.' Hitler's only reply was, 'I do not wish to make a peace founded on vengeance.'

These words of mine were published during the Occupation in an interview which I gave in May 1941 to the United Press. They show that I did not humble myself before the conqueror. And I wish to emphasise that I never conceived as a just peace one which would surrender a single inch of our homeland or of our Empire.

Hitler's reference to 'economic collaboration' was not discussed at Montoire as it had been agreed that the Marshal would reserve his position for discussion with his ministers before coming to any agreement. This position was set forth in the communiqué which the Marshal published after the interview.

'Collaboration' has now come to be a byword and is taken to describe French policy after Montoire. But these activities, which were once called 'collaboration', described to-day as 'intelligence with the enemy' were, in fact, prescribed in the Armistice Convention.

Not only is the principle of economic collaboration imposed in this Convention, but even the word 'collaboration' is used. Article 3 of the Convention begins as follows: 'In the occupied areas of France the German Reich will exercise all the rights of an occupying power; the French Government undertakes to facilitate by every possible means the implementation of its rights and to execute the decisions of the occupying power through its administrative machinery. The French Government instructs all French authorities and all the administrative services in the occupied territories to conform faithfully to the regulations issued by the German military authorities and *to collaborate* with the latter in a correct manner.' (Italics by Pierre Laval.)

There can be no doubt, therefore, that with this text before them the Germans were in a position to require collaboration in theory and in practice from the French Government and its public services.

They made full use of this provision and as the Occupation extended and their needs increased they soon reached the point where this Article 3, which was cited whenever they wished to make a new demand upon us, was freely used by them to justify every form of abuse.

It is easy for those plenipotentiaries who went to Rethondes to say to-day that this Armistice Convention was forced on us, but is it not somewhat illogical for the very men who agreed to these terms to attack those who afterwards were obliged to respect the agreements to which they had subscribed?

It was not Montoire which inaugurated a policy of collaboration. This policy was forced upon us by the Armistice Convention.

There were many abuses; could they have been prevented? During four years of ceaseless struggle the French Government daily and hourly fought to reduce and to minimise the German demands.

Had the Armistice lasted only a few weeks, or at most a few months, we should not have had to undergo such harshness from the occupying power. But the Armistice lasted four long years, and we had no means, no weapons, other than negotiations described to-day as 'intelligence with the enemy', to serve as a barrier to German cruelty and rapacity.

The most lurid violation of the Armistice Convention was the crossing of the demarcation line by the German army on 11 November 1942. When I protested, the Germans replied that we had violated the first and third paragraphs of the Armistice Convention, which read as follows:

'1. *The French Government undertakes to engage in no hostile acts against the German Reich with any part of its remaining armed forces or in any other manner.*'

'3. *The French Government will order its citizens to refrain from taking up arms against Germany in the service of States with which Germany is at war. Those of French nationality who fail to comply with this undertaking will be treated by the German troops as francs-tireurs.*'

The military developments in North Africa marked, without any doubt, the point of departure for our liberation, but this argument was not very convincing to the Germans at that time. We had no means of breaking the Armistice and no matter what hardships ensued we could not abandon France to the whims of a conqueror whose harshness increased in proportion to his military difficulties.

Astonishment has been expressed that the Government failed to resign on 8 November 1942, and that the Marshal and I failed to proceed to Algiers. No one has asked what would have happened if the leaders in Algiers, instead of abusing us day and night on their radios, had made some attempt to establish contact with us.

We might have found the necessary formula for agreement, that is, between those who were fighting abroad for the liberation of France and those who, in France, were making every effort to save what could be saved. I have no doubt that this agreement might have been effected, because it was in the interest of our country that it should have been effected.*

It was suggested to me at that time that I should leave. It was even suggested that I should thus acquire popularity, but when I explained to those who made the suggestion what the consequences of such action would be they replied: 'You are absolutely right. You must remain.'

* It is interesting to note that Hitler himself, after talking to Laval at Montoire, seems have thought that there was a secret understanding between Pétain, Laval, Weygand and de Gaulle. The reader will find in Appendix XI Hitler's comment, made on November 18, 1940, one month after Montoire, at Berchtesgaden, and reported by Serrano Suñer, Spain's former Minister of Foreign Affairs.

In fact, for example, on 11 November 1942, after long and protracted discussions, I obtained the German agreement to leave unmolested the citizens of Alsace and Lorraine who had taken refuge in the Southern Zone of France. I obtained the same agreement for the 80,000 escaped prisoners who were in the South and the 650,000 prisoners who were on leave from captivity.

Had I abandoned my post in November 1942 the whole of the country would have become one vast *maquis*. The cost would have been thousands and thousands of dead. It is understandable that brave men and true patriots did not hesitate to expose themselves to the consequences of Article 10, which outlawed them as guerillas or francs-tireurs. But how could the head of the Government be justified in taking a decision which would expose the entire French population to this terrible risk? Had the Armistice Convention not existed we should not have had to apply it and to suffer the incalculable abuses demanded in its name, but this is merely theoretical. Even though I believed at the time the Armistice was signed that it was indispensable in the French interest, I held this opinion in common with 99 per cent of the French people, but, I repeat, my personal opinion had no influence on the decision which was taken by the Government before its arrival at Bordeaux. This point was clearly brought out at the Pétain trial.

As Minister I was subsequently obliged to take into account the Armistice Convention, but I shall establish, without any possibility of refutation, that I did everything in my power to weaken its impact, notably each time the Germans attempted to stretch it in order to justify some activity or to violate and aggravate its terms.

CHAPTER 8

13 DECEMBER 1940

WHEN I was in Paris on 12 December as Minister of Foreign Affairs in Marshal Pétain's Government I received a visit from Herr Abetz, the German Ambassador. He informed me that Hitler had decided to restore to France the ashes of Napoleon's son, the 'Aiglon'. The ceremony was to take place at the Invalides on Saturday, 14th, and Marshal Pétain was invited to be present. The Ambassador went on to say that as this gesture of Hitler had a high political significance the Führer hoped that it would be understood and appreciated in France 'as an act of sympathy, of great historical importance'. He added that the gesture underlined Hitler's desire to create a spirit of reconciliation between the two countries. He pointed out that the Marshal would thus have the first opportunity since the Armistice of establishing contact with the people of Paris and of presiding at a national ceremony. He then handed me Hitler's letter of invitation which I was to transmit to the Marshal. This conversation took place at the Hôtel Matignon.

I told Herr Abetz that as it was already 12 December the period given to the Marshal was very short, the day set forth for the ceremony being only two days off. I said that the Marshal was old and the weather extremely cold and that all this might prevent his accepting an invitation so suddenly tendered. I promised, however, to telephone at once to Vichy and to inform the Ambassador of the Marshal's reply.

It was M. Dumoulin de la Barthète who answered and took my message. He called me back a little later to say that the Marshal was not in a position to answer such an invitation, the suddenness of which made it discourteous. He stated that a person of the Marshal's age and rank should not be so treated and that his state of health rendered the trip to Paris impossible. He added that the Marshal himself would fix the date which he deemed fitting for his entry into Paris, and that as he had not been previously informed of the return of the 'Aiglon's' ashes he would not attend the ceremony.

I at once informed Abetz, who came back to see me at the Hôtel Matignon. He told me that he personally regretted that the invitation had been made so late but that he had transmitted it immediately upon receipt. According to Abetz, it was Hitler's way to take rapid decisions. He begged me to retain only the friendly intention which had inspired it and added that a refusal such as I was transmitting—of which, however, I had slightly softened the terms—might result in grave consequences. He became most insistent, begging me to persuade the Marshal to reconsider the matter in order not to complicate and poison Franco-German relations.

I could only agree to pass on this communication to the Marshal. Before receiving the Marshal's final reply I had sent for the Government's representative in Paris, General de la Laurencie, and the Prefect of Police, M. Langeron, in order to discuss whether the Marshal, in the event of his acceptance, should stay at the Elysée or in Versailles. In either case the problem of heating had to be attended to immediately. General de la Laurencie made it very plain that he disapproved the journey proposed for the Marshal and his attendance at a ceremony where German officers and soldiers would doubtless be present. I could merely confirm the communications as I received them.

I was advised, shortly after, that for purely material reasons it would not be possible for the Marshal to reside either in Versailles or at the Elysée so I decided to turn over to him the Hôtel Matignon, where I was staying, in case he chose to come.

My interview with Abetz and the scarcely veiled threat about the grave consequences which might result if the Marshal refused led me to go at once to Vichy. I deemed it my duty to explain the situation fully to the Marshal in person so that whatever decision he was eventually to reach should be his alone. De Brinon, who had been present at my conversations with Abetz, accompanied me.

We reached Vichy on Friday 13 December at about quarter to one. I met the Marshal, who was returning from his walk, and we made an appointment for three o'clock.

Our conversation lasted until 3.45. I repeated Abetz's exact words and was much surprised by the difference between the Marshal's own attitude and that described by Dumoulin de la Barthète when transmitting the Marshal's refusal the day before. The Marshal agreed to come to Paris and informed me of his intention to stay at the Hôtel Matignon; he even decided on a small official lunch. Our conversation was characterised by the utmost cordiality. I returned to my office, where I received Señor de Lequerica, the Spanish Ambassador, and afterwards presided at the Cabinet Council at five o'clock. All the ministers were present, with the exception of M. Alibert.

Afterwards I went to M. Dumoulin de la Barthète's office. He was to give me the Marshal's written answer to Hitler. I read the letter and simply observed that the terms of formal politeness chosen were neither opportune nor according to official protocol. The Marshal had assured the Chancellor of 'ses meilleurs sentiments'. I suggested the official protocol formula, 'ses sentiments de haute considération'.

While I was in Dumoulin's office, General Laure entered and announced that the Council of Ministers was to take place at eight o'clock. I did not know that this meeting had been called. M. Dumoulin de la Barthète feigned the same ignorance. I suppose that the Marshal wished to inform the ministers of his departure for Paris.

I had scarcely entered the Council Room when the Marshal came in, accompanied by M. Baudouin. He was extremely pale and nervous. He said, 'I wish each minister to sign and hand in his resignation.'

We all signed, and I thought that the Marshal, who at the

time was in disagreement with M. Belin, then Minister of Labour, wished to designate his successor. The Marshal retired for a few minutes, during which I learned nothing from the other ministers, whose attitude appeared to me rather strange.

The Marshal then returned and announced: 'The resignations of M. Laval and of M. Ripert are the only ones accepted.' Thereupon I asked him to explain the reasons for such a sudden decision, more especially as his attitude during our conversation a few hours before had been particularly cordial and friendly. He answered that he could never tell each time I went to Paris what bad news I would bring back, that I had put obstacles in the way of his installation at Versailles and that I had inspired the articles written by M. Déat against his ministers. I replied that he was always given a full account of my trips to Paris, that it was not, alas, in my power to prevent the Germans from taking decisions which were disagreeable to us, that on the contrary I spent my whole time intervening to prevent such action. I had done everything in my power to facilitate his installation at Versailles, which up to then had been postponed by the Germans, and that I had nothing whatever to do with Déat's articles. My last words were: 'I hope that your successive and contradictory decisions will not cause too much harm to our country.'

I then returned to my office where I informed my assistants of my departure and got together my business and personal papers. Great animation reigned throughout the Hôtel du Parc. I was informed that the corridors were crowded with police, particularly a police of a new sort called G.P. (Groupe de Protection, recruited from among the 'Cagoule'). M. Rochat, General Secretary of Foreign Affairs, was with me. Dr. Ménétrel and M. Dumoulin de la Barthète kept coming in and out without being able to explain (at least that is what they told me) the reason which had led the Marshal to take this decision. All telephone communications had been severed. I remembered that I was able to put a call through to

Chateldon immediately upon my entering my office, but that after that I was unable to obtain any other communication.

My intention had been to return that night to my Paris home with my wife and daughter. A train left at about midnight. My car was to follow, with my baggage and papers, which were packed.

At about 10.30 an American journalist, Ralph Heinzen, United Press representative in France, reached my office with difficulty. He had been jostled and rather roughly handled. Only his repeated statement that he was an American newspaper-man had enabled him to force his way up. He told me that my chauffeur had been arrested and the car taken. I then realised that the Marshal's action was accompanied by police measures and that I should be prevented from going to Paris. At the same moment, M. Mondanel, Director of the National Police, invited me to follow him, stating that he had been ordered to escort me to Chateldon. I requested him to exhibit his orders. He complied and I did not insist any further except to inquire of General Laure, upon whose initiative he had acted and who had signed the papers. 'It is in accordance with the Marshal's order,' was General Laure's reply.

It was under these conditions and with strong police escort that I was taken to Chateldon where my home was already heavily guarded by mobile forces. Police inspectors were installed in the house and I obtained from M. Mondanel an order that they should not enter my bedroom. The telephone had been cut, no visit was authorised, nor could I leave the premises. My wife was obliged to submit to the same vexations, and so was my daughter, who had just arrived from New York.

Neither my wife nor my daughter had been there when I was brought home. As soon as they saw the police arrive they became anxious. They had not been able to gather the slightest information from the officers or men, who were completely ignorant of what was going on. They had, therefore, gone immediately to Vichy and called at M. Heinzen's office. He had informed them and they had returned to join me at Chateldon.

Doubtless as the result of an oversight, our radio had been left. Next morning, the 14th, I heard the Marshal's statement that he had parted from me for 'reasons of internal policy'. The exact terms of the declaration can be found in the newspapers of that date. I believe that it was on the Sunday morning that I heard a broadcast from Paris describing the ceremony at the Invalides (Admiral Darlan represented the Marshal), de Brinon was mentioned as having attended. On the next day, Monday morning, two senior officers passed in front of my door; I inquired what they wanted. 'We came to inspect the premises because you are about to receive a visit,' was their reply. I was unable to ascertain who the visitor was to be.

On the next day, Tuesday morning, at nine o'clock, the 'Commissaire Divisionnaire', Head of the Police, informed me that all orders had been cancelled by the Government and that I was free.

An hour or two later, at about eleven, M. Dumoulin de la Barthète arrived and asked me if I could come to Vichy and talk to the Marshal. He told me that Abetz was there. I entered his car with him (mine was to be returned to me at Vichy). During the drive I asked him to give me the reasons for this odious and burlesque adventure. After evading several of my questions he ended by saying: 'It's that idiot Alibert, who succeeded in making the Marshal believe that you wanted to lure him into a trap in Paris with the intention of having him arrested.'

I believe he subsequently denied making this statement, but my memory is very faithful. It was just after passing through the village of Saint-Yorre that he said those words, which were to me so strange and unexpected.

On arriving at the *Pavillon Sévigné* I was immediately led into the Marshal's office. Darlan was beside him, and without any explanation the Marshal offered me the post of Minister of the Interior. I refused and remember saying, with some bitterness, 'I have to thank you for the treatment you inflicted upon my wife and daughter.' He answered: 'I know nothing of all this.' Later, I talked with Abetz, who I thought might be in a position to explain some of the happenings, as I knew that he and the Marshal had had a conversation which lasted all morning.

I was able to learn that immediately after my arrest all my assistants had been closely guarded at pistol point in their own rooms. The German Embassy in Paris had had the greatest difficulty in obtaining telephonic communication with Vichy. The Marshal denied having had anything to do with my arrest. He told Abetz that there had been a gross misunderstanding and that his intention was to offer me the Ministry of the Interior.

The Ambassador pointed out that all these events had taken place at the time of Hitler's invitation and were criticised severely in Berlin. He added that if the Marshal had had any serious reasons for grievance against me he should not have entrusted me with the post of Minister of Foreign Affairs, which placed me in direct contact with the German Embassy, still less should he have entrusted me with the Montoire negotiations with Chancellor Hitler.

'President Laval interests us only inasmuch as he represents you,' Abetz went on to say. He added that, after conferring with the Marshal, he was of the opinion that this whole affair had been staged by the Marshal's immediate entourage, and that it was the Marshal's duty to put his own house in order if he wished to have normal relations with the German Government.

I saw the Marshal again on the same day. Once more he had changed his mind. He offered me the choice between the Ministry of Agriculture and that of Industrial Production. Our conversation was rather animated, especially on my side. I refused to work with him and made use of rather strong language concerning the measures taken against me.

I was about to leave Vichy and return to Chateldon when

the German Ambassador requested an appointment for late afternoon. He came to see me, accompanied by Dumoulin de la Barthète, but did not tell me anything new, though he had lunched with the Marshal. I learned later from the French police, who had guarded me the day before, that on Thursday the 19th the official guard was to have been changed for a section of G.P. (*Groupe de Protection*) and that a certain Norey was commissioned to shoot me on the false pretext that I was trying to escape.

It is true that, following 13 December, certain newspapers in Paris launched a campaign to protest against my removal from the Government. This was quite natural and any other attitude would have been surprising in view of the fact that it was generally believed that my misfortune had been the result of the decision of the Marshal to break with the Montoire policy, and particularly as it was known in Paris that, at the time of my arrest, I was on the verge of obtaining tangible results, notably the release of prisoners and the solution of other problems which, just then, were vital to the welfare of our country, such as the reintegration of the Northern and Pas-de-Calais departments into the administrative control of Paris, a drastic reduction of the cost of occupation and a more flexible handling of the barrier at the line of demarcation.

Von Ribbentrop was to have communicated to me the German offer on these points some time before 25 December, probably on the 22nd. The group of French journalists, which had recently returned to Paris, even discounting the fact that they were already under German influence, could only regret and be indignant that a result so promising should have been compromised.

As for the German Embassy and its staff, they were naturally surprised by this development because they had assumed up to then that the Marshal was in agreement with this policy. They regarded as offensive all the pretexts which were invoked to justify this break. In their view the Marshal should have carefully weighed his opinion of me before entrusting me officially with the mission of representing the French Government *vis-à-vis* the German Government. If I was, in his eyes, unworthy of this trust, the Marshal should have reached this conclusion before he placed me in contact with the Minister of Foreign Affairs and the Chancellor of the German Reich. These were, I believe, the views which the responsible German authorities in France expressed at that time.

In any event, this campaign lasted only a short while because the Germans came to the conclusion that they would have better success in their negotiations with Admiral Darlan than they could have had with me.*

From the time they received from the Marshal and the Admiral assurances that there would be no modification of the policy of agreement with Germany and that, on the contrary, 'collaboration' would be accentuated, the German services made it evident that they were totally satisfied. They did not really wish me to replace Admiral Darlan and they did not conceal their viewpoint from those who had occasion to have contact with them.

Admiral Darlan remained in office one year and three months and Germany obtained from him concessions in the naval, military, and economic fields which I should never have proposed or accepted under any circumstances. In this connection, during the Pétain trial, I recapitulated several decisions made in 1941 in judicial and police affairs that were to weigh heavily on the Government, which I afterwards headed.

In order to place the charges made against me in their proper perspective and to prove how false they are, I must here emphasise that before the war I had no contact whatso-

* This statement on Darlan by Pierre Laval was confirmed two years after Laval's death when the British Admiralty published in London, in 1947, the report of Admiral Schultze to Admiral Raedar, dated December 3rd, 1941, showing how far Admiral Darlan was willing to go in making concessions in the military and naval fields.

ever with Abetz, although this gentleman moved in wide
circles in the political and press world of Paris. I never set
eyes upon him before our first meeting, which took place on
his initiative on 20 July 1940.

Furthermore, I had not known the German Ambassador
who had preceded him at the Embassy in the Rue de Lille.
My only relations with the German Embassy occurred when
I was Minister of Foreign Affairs and then they were on an
official plane, with von Hoesch in 1931 and with Koester in
1935. I have never been present at a luncheon or at a reception at the German Embassy. In particular, I did not attend,
although I was invited, the great reception which was given
by the German Embassy when von Ribbentrop visited Paris
officially to sign an agreement with M. Georges Bonnet.

In 1934, when I was Minister of Foreign Affairs, I received
Herr von Ribbentrop at the Quai d'Orsay. At that time he
was not a minister and I received him at the specific request
of Koester, then the German Ambassador. He was introduced
to me as a sort of semi-official envoy of Hitler. I met Goering
at Cracow in 1935 during the funeral services of Marshal
Pilsudski. Both these men complained bitterly of my diplomatic activities and reproached me with practising a policy
which tended to encircle the Reich. Goering observed: 'We
find your hand wherever plots are hatched against Germany.'
The record of this conversation, drafted by M. Rochat, who
attended, may be found at the Quai d'Orsay. My agreements
with Rome, as well as the Franco-Soviet pact, caused them
acute embarrassment and they did not disguise their irrita-
tion, which was reflected in the Press.

In 1935 the Austrian Chancellor, Schuschnigg, visited me
in Paris. The purpose of his visit was to request the aid and
protection of France against Hitler. The malevolence of certain political parties at that time was such that I had to
receive him in a suburban station outside of Paris because
a demonstration had been organised by the Communists and
Socialists in the centre of town against his visit and the

policy which it betokened. The Germans were fully aware that all my activities were directed towards setting up a barrier to prevent the fulfilment of Hitler's ambitions.

Following the signing of the treaty with Italy, Herr von Hassel, the German Ambassador to Rome, stated to me at the Venetian Palace, in the presence of Mussolini: 'Some day Germany will be forced to come to an agreement with you because alone you cannot hope to stand up against the whole world.' I need not remark that a statement of this sort, made at such a time and under such circumstances, was faithfully reported to Berlin. This statement in particular created a sensation, because it was overheard and repeated.

All this goes to prove that I was not regarded in Berlin as a statesman who could be counted upon to endure the German hegemony in Europe that was bound to result from the breaking of the chain which I had welded around the Reich in 1935 with such pains, at a time when it was isolated in Europe.

In 1936 and 1939, when I was no longer at the Quai d'Orsay, I took an active part in the deliberations of the Committee of Foreign Affairs of the Senate. If one reads to-day the records of the secret sessions of this body, which I shall make available during my trial, all my views will appear crystal clear. These views never changed. I knew that we were in danger of war. Hitler did not conceal either his ambitions nor the extent of his armaments, which increased in equal measure. As a Senator I made frantic appeals for action, appeals such as no other man then in power, in Russia, England, America, or France, uttered at that time.

Our break with Italy upset the balance of Europe, and Hitler, from then on, eagerly seized every occasion to set Europe on fire. The annexation of Austria and the invasion of Czechoslovakia were thus facilitated; the invasion of Poland was to follow.

At the time, I protested vigorously against the humiliation of Munich. I did not wait, as some have done, until Germany was defeated before recording my views. I shall read at my trial a statement which I made on 16 March 1939 at a secret session of the Committee of Foreign Affairs of the Senate in the presence of Georges Bonnet, then Minister of Foreign Affairs in the Daladier Government. The terms which I then used to denounce the German peril are therein clearly set forth. (See Pierre Laval's statement, Appendix IV.)

I have been blamed by Parliament and Press for failing to apply the sanctions against Italy with sufficient emphasis at the time of the Ethiopian war. I took note of and replied to these charges in a speech I made to the Chamber on 28 December 1935, following which I obtained a vote of confidence.

Some say that I have been lenient towards Italy because of its Fascist Government. This assertion is absurd; it was put forth for certain internal political purposes which I need not dwell upon here.

In this connection it will perhaps be interesting to re-read at this time the explanations I gave as Prime Minister before the Chamber in November 1935 in defending my domestic policies which had saved the franc. Our financial situation was then such as to render possible the conversion of our Government bonds, and a renewed turning of the wheels of production took place only five minutes after we had faced complete catastrophe. Who led the attack on me that day? The same who attacked me one month later with regard to my foreign policy. From Léon Blum to Marcel Déat there was a solid front. I shall make only one comment in rejecting this charge of my alleged leniency towards the Italian form of government: in the same year in which I came to terms with Italy, I made an agreement with Soviet Russia. In Rome I saw the Pope and Mussolini; several weeks later in Moscow I saw Stalin.

I have been accused of lacking ideals, doubtless because I have always believed and still believe that foreign policy, though it must take into account certain imponderables, should be based on solid realities. Regimes follow one another in solemn procession, governments undergo revolu-

tions, but geography remains invariable. We shall be neighbours of Germany for ever.

I do possess an ideal: it is peace. If we do not find means
of establishing good neighbourly relations with Germany so
that we can live together side by side, war will return inevitably and periodically. This is a difficult problem to solve,
but those who have the responsibility of governing our country must face and solve it. Such is their solemn duty.

The tragedy is that the German people look upon war as a
perfectly natural thing and peace as an accident. The further
tragedy is that they too willingly place their destiny in the
hands of those who lead them along the path of adventure.
A still further tragedy is Germany's ferocious pride. A final
tragedy is that the Germans look upon themselves as a
chosen people. It has been the fashion to say: 'There are two
Germanys.' This unfortunately is not the case. There is
only one Germany, and she always follows the chiefs she
chooses to lead her.

Like certain others, I sought in the period between the
two wars to solve the difficult problem of our relations with
Germany. I accompanied M. Briand to Berlin in 1931.
Germany at that time had a parliamentary form of government and the head of the Government, Brüning, was a Catholic. Both on the French and on the German side we were
convinced of the necessity of a reconciliation and of reaching
an agreement, but public opinion is capricious.

'We shall never make the same gestures and pronounce the
same words at the same time,' Brüning told me in a voice
which was tinged with sadness and disillusion.

Then came Hitler. The problem remained as before, but
in attempting to solve it with Hitler in power other methods
had to be employed; to German force a greater force had to
be opposed, a union of all those whom he threatened. A
solid chain had to be forged in order to avoid catastrophe,
that is to say before the war, to prevent war with its far-reaching and disastrous consequences for France. This was the

policy which I sponsored. It was a difficult one. There was a conflict between patriotism and certain ideologies.

It was a pastime of many of our fellow-citizens to concern themselves rather with the internal regimes of other countries than with the natural frontiers of France. Such was the case in 1936 during the Ethiopian war. It was again the case, though in reverse, when the Soviet Union allied itself with Germany. This move might have been foreseen; for if Stalin has a powerful ideal which extends into and permeates all countries of the world, he possesses also a strong sense of reality.

My attempts in 1931 to find a basis of agreement with Germany in a policy of reconciliation had gained for me, among our neighbours, the reputation of a man of goodwill. I had also inherited, to a lesser degree of course, some of Briand's halo, so that, in the words of Goering, I represented to the Germans 'an honest enemy'. It is not, therefore, surprising that much less antipathy attached to my name than to the names of certain other French political personalities.

I had stood up to Hitler at Montoire, using terms which impressed him as coming from a man who evidently was not a coward and whom, in consequence, he held in esteem. It would be unworthy of me to contrast the conversation which I had with Hitler with the language used by the Marshal when speaking to him two days later.

We were then defeated and in 1940 I did not believe that the defeat of Germany was probable. My duty was to reduce as much as possible the financial burden of our country, which was the consequence of our defeat. I was determined that we should not abandon one square inch of our homeland or of our Empire. Without us, Germany could not possibly organise Europe and it was clear to me that she would have to pay, in terms of our independence and our territorial integrity, a price for our co-operation, a co-operation which was wholly indispensable to her in the reconstruction of Europe.

I had been accustomed, in speaking to the Germans when we were the masters, to use language which they understood and could not, now that we were suffering every humiliation, bring myself to speak to Hitler in different terms. Had the war ended at this time or at any time while Germany was allied to the Soviet Union, we should have had less to fear from German ambition. We should have been in a position to strike a balance of power by playing the Russian hand if Germany had attempted to establish her hegemony in Europe.

In reviewing these past events, particularly those which immediately preceded 13 December, a reply is made to the unfair charges of the Accusation, which suggest the idea that there was some obscure and unknown reason why—to quote the text of this charge—I suddenly became 'the man who, in France, Germany preferred above all others and in whom she placed the greatest confidence'.

CHAPTER 9

WHY I RETURNED TO OFFICE IN THE SPRING OF 1942

A TALK WITH GOERING

A T Marshal Pétain's trial I recited certain facts which completely destroy the allegation that 'I returned to office through connivance, and with the support of the occupying power'.

I was deeply wounded by the odious and ridiculous measures which were taken against me on 13 December, and, above all, indignant at the calumnies spread throughout the country intended to create an impression that I had used my office to make concessions to the Germans of which the Marshal was ignorant. This perfidious campaign was led for the most part by individuals or groups financed directly by the Marshal's office, and it is no exaggeration to say that their means for spreading propaganda of this sort were exceedingly impressive. The object of this campaign was to prove that the step taken on 13 December had become imperative and that the concessions which the Government had been obliged to make to the Germans after my dismissal were less damaging than they would have been had I remained in office. Meanwhile, with true duplicity, they explained to the Germans that, now I was out of the way, the Government would go considerably further on the road of collaboration, as it was I who had prevented the Marshal from doing all he wished to do along this line. While I was out of office the Marshal's Government proved, in the naval, military, and civil domains, how far it would go in the direction of collaboration.

One might say that it would have been a natural thing

to me to try to return to office in order to achieve revenge
and justify myself. Had I really been animated by these
considerations I should have had an easy opportunity on 17
December 1940, four days after the notorious 'affair of 13
December'.

On that day the Marshal offered me my choice of three
Cabinet posts. Because it followed the insult of which I
had been victim I turned down this offer with disgust. This
goes to prove that I was not looking for any ministerial post.
I rejected these offers in spite of a natural temptation to
prove to public opinion that I was the victim of the contradictory whims of the Marshal.

My plan for our relations with Germany contained no
hint of subordination. My statements made to the Paris
Press on 1 November 1940, immediately after the meeting
at Montoire, prove that my Government intended to face
the Germans with its hands absolutely free. 'Some day France
will understand the nature and extent of the efforts which
this Government has made,' I observed at that time; 'we
shall be judged on the basis of the results which we have
obtained.'

Several hundred thousand prisoners of war paid in terms
of continued captivity for the political blunder of 13 December, and the financial structure of our country had to
bear the enormous burden of the Occupation cost which,
had not this blunder been made, would have been reduced
from 400 million to 180 million francs per day.

The decision of 13 December broke up a policy which
should have been followed as long as it was profitable to
France. A little band of men void of any political experience
or political principle, real sorcerer's apprentices, then began
to play their little game of internal politics without realising
that it would be our country as a whole which would have
to pay, our prisoners and our finances, and that finally our
remaining shred of liberty, which we were trying so hard to
preserve, would be destroyed by their crazy and childish
undertaking.

The United States was, at that time, far from entering the war. The Soviet Union was the ally of Germany. It was quite possible to conceive a profitable negotiation through which France, wounded and bleeding though she was, might recover and preserve her position in the world. Was I wrong? Now that Germany has been defeated militarily and the regime whose powers for destruction could not then be accurately measured has fallen, people may say that I was wrong. In those days, however, there was no other way to reduce the destructive power of that machine; the more terrible it was, the greater was our duty to save what we could of wounded France during those long hard years.

The least that can be said about 'the coup of 13 December' is that it lost for France substantial advantages which Germany later could not easily have taken away from us.

On the very eve of this memorable day the full measure of the mistake which had been made could be taken. For five long months the Prefects of the Northern Zone had to wait before it was possible for them to consult with the ministers in Vichy. With the exception of Admiral Darlan, none of the ministers in Vichy could cross the line in the direction of Paris. The German pressure on the French administrative bodies constantly increased and, in order to breathe more freely, the French Government had to make sacrifice upon sacrifice and furnish ransom after ransom. This was Darlan's policy.

I have already shown what concessions the Admiral of the Fleet was obliged to make in the fields of justice and of the police, and I have described the chains in which we were then bound.

Why should I have wished to return to power in 1942 when events were of this kind? It is my firm belief that, although the German Government treated me with courtesy, it did not wish to see me enter again the field of negotiation; I believe that even my political adversaries will grant me this. I was very much worried about my pledges made to the National Assembly on 10 July 1940, but I was confident that whatever the ambitions of Admiral Darlan might be he would not permit any action directed by the Marshal or his entourage against the Republic and Republican Government. Admiral Darlan had always lived and moved in parliamentary circles and claimed that he was a sincere Republican. I was ready to believe him, particularly as he assured me that his sole desire was to become President of the Republic when conditions should warrant such a nomination.

After February 1941 I had no contact either with the Marshal or Darlan, nor did I visit Vichy until my return to office in 1942. I lived in Paris and for frequent periods stayed at my home at Chateldon. I lived very much alone, received few visitors and engaged in no activity which in any way might have contributed to my return to power.

As a consequence, it is necessary to look elsewhere for the reasons which motivated my return to office and which refute conclusively this charge based on a hypothesis which is not borne out by the facts.

In March 1942 I met a certain Colonel Knochen in Paris and took this opportunity to express my astonishment at the worsening of our relations with Germany and in particular at the drastic measures which the Germans were imposing upon France with increasing severity.

'I regret very much', I remarked, 'that I am not in a position to repeat this statement to a responsible German official.' Thereupon he asked me to defer my return to Chateldon, which I had told him was imminent. This was on a Thursday. On the following Saturday he informed me that Marshal Goering would be in Paris and that I should have an opportunity of meeting him.

The Colonel was most insistent that I should refrain from mentioning the possibility of this meeting to anyone. He came himself on Saturday with another man, whom I was given to understand was Goering's nephew, to conduct me to Goering. He escorted me to the Quai d'Orsay and I was led into the office which I had occupied so frequently. There

I found Goering and General Hanesse, the former German Air Attaché in Paris, who was to serve as interpreter.

Goering said that our meeting should be considered strictly confidential. He wished the knowledge of it to be withheld even from the German Embassy. He agreed at the close, however, that I might mention it to Marshal Pétain, but to him alone.

I had to listen to a violent diatribe against France. 'We were bitterly mistaken when we thought that we could work out a sincere collaboration with your country,' he said in substance. 'We have seen the light and know now that we were mistaken. Henceforth we shall treat France with the same hostility that she has manifested so clearly against us.'

He complained, moreover, about the Saint Florentin conversations. Goering was extremely irritable, and each time I protested he redoubled his accusations against the French Government, the activities of the French people, and the trend of French public opinion.

He did not specifically mention Poland and the harsh regime which Germany had imposed on that pathetic country, but his bitter language and his outright accusations made me understand that we were to be treated in the same ruthless manner.

I attempted to urge that there must not be any irreconcilable misunderstanding between our two countries because of the future. I argued that if a little goodwill were shown, lasting peace might be achieved between us and that even the problem of Alsace-Lorraine was not insoluble. I said that the burden of organising the whole of Europe fell on Germany and France. For Germany, as well as for France, I emphasised, a sincere and lasting peace was vitally necessary. He replied brutally that Germany's experience with France had been conclusive and that thereafter France would be treated in the way she deserved.

I was impressed by the advice which he gave me at the close of our conversation. 'If the Marshal should ask you to return to office,' Goering said, 'refuse. For a man like you it would be far too late and much too soon. Towards us you have shown a consistent but honest enmity. Perhaps some day after the war, when peace has been restored and you can defend the interests of your country, we shall meet again.'

Two salient facts remained graven in my mind after this meeting. The Occupation was to become immeasurably more severe and if Germany should be victorious the terms of peace would be harsh.

As I said at the Pétain trial, I reported this conversation to the Marshal. This was the purpose of our meeting in the forest at Randan. The 'two-face' policy, which was the basis of the Marshal's defence, had clearly been neither very successful nor skilfully carried out. The result had been a failure. The Marshal was overcome by Goering's statements, which I quoted and which evidently were a total surprise. At that time he was living in Vichy in an atmosphere of illusion intensified by the public adulation which surrounded him.

The Marshal asked my advice and begged me to help him. He urged me to receive Admiral Darlan to acquaint him with the details of my conversation with Goering and to concert a policy with him.

Even then I did not know that the S.S. units had recently been moved to France and that we were on the eve of a veritable siege directed by Gauleiter Sauckel. I knew only that we had not suffered the last degradation and that we had far from drained the dregs of our bitter cup.

At my first meeting with Darlan, which took place at Chateldon, the Admiral asked me, on behalf of the Marshal, to re-enter the Government. I refused. All the members of my family, without exception, begged me not to return to power.

At no time in my life was my conscience so deeply troubled. Sometimes it is difficult to find and follow the true path of duty. I understood and sympathised with the objections which my dear ones raised. It was impossible at that time to inform French public opinion of the truth and I might be accused, later on, of having some part of the responsibility for the evil demands and deeds of the Germans.

But did I have the right to consider my personal interests when my duty towards my country was in the balance? I knew that I should feel extremely guilty were I to fail in action or in word to diminish even to a small extent the misery of France and of the French people.

At this point Admiral Darlan was guilty of a grave tactical mistake. He revealed to the Germans a telegram which he had received from Washington, but in doing so he changed and added to the text. From that moment his situation was untenable.

After I returned to the Government, General Hanesse, whom I had to meet in Paris, expressed Marshal Goering's extreme surprise that I should have taken this step in spite of our conversation, the statements he had made, and the advice he had given me. I believe that a French witness, who was playing a double game which was intelligent and useful to France, will bear out everything that I have said above. This Frenchman, a leading industrialist, was arrested later, and I had the greatest difficulty before I left Paris in bringing about his release by the German secret police, which had learned that he belonged to the Resistance.*

Had I been able, in 1942, to tell the truth to the French people there would have been no misunderstanding then, and there would be no misunderstanding now, as to the extent of the sacrifice which I resolved to make in order to defend their interests.

It is only necessary to read the Prosecutor's Accusation against me to understand the violence of the hatred with which I was pursued by a great number of my fellow-citizens. When the facts are known, when the results of my policy are listed and the circumstances are explained, when the ghosts of misunderstanding and ignorance are laid, the full extent of

---

* The industrialist here mentioned is M. Outhenin-Chalandre, who was subsequently made Commander of the Legion of Honour after the Liberation.

my sacrifice will appear. The full measure of my love for my country, without which I could not have undertaken such a thankless task, will then be recognised.

I had no responsibility for our defeat. I had no responsibility for the conduct of the war. I was not responsible for the failure of the policy which I inaugurated at Montoire to spare France as many of the bitter fruits of defeat as possible. Nevertheless, at this late hour I decided to face the risks and perils of a mission which might result in some lightehing of the heavy burden of suffering which had been laid on the people of France.

This is the root and basis of my whole answer to the Prosecutor.

If what I stated is true there can be no justification for the charges brought against me unless those who persecuted me are fearful of enlightening a public opinion from which the truth has been withheld.

If the people of France are permitted to learn the facts in my case and if they believe that my presentation of them is honest and sincere how can they condemn me?

How can my statements be doubted when it is so easy to see the many grounds on which I might have declined the Marshal's appeal to return to office?

I had no personal feeling of attachment towards him. I had been his victim. I had been severely critical of the political blunders of which he was guilty in the exercise of a high office which he often regarded as a means of satisfying his personal preferences. It is true that in July 1940 I had shared with many others the responsibility of granting him extraordinary powers, but the brutal police action which he took against me on 13 December released me from any obligation which I had previously assumed to remain in office in order to defend the Republic. I felt sure that Darlan, would in any event, respect this obligation.

It was not difficult for me to prove, merely by contrasting the policy which I had proposed in 1940 with the unhappy results of the policy which had been followed since my departure, that I had been right and that the Marshal and Darlan had been wrong. I had fully recovered from the wound to my self-esteem which I had suffered on 13 December.

To sum up, every personal reason was against my return to power, and no good reason except a patriotic one in favour of it. The Germans had made it crystal clear that they were not disposed to modify their attitude favourably, and everything except patriotism urged me to escape responsibility in a situation which appeared insoluble.

The statement I made before the Judge in my preliminary hearing with regard to the warnings which the S.S. Chief Heydrich made to M. Bousquet, the Secretary of our Police, on 5 May 1942, that is to say, several days after my return, illuminates the fearful circumstances—in using this word 'fearful' I do not exaggerate—under which I resumed public office.

For one thing, no sooner had I taken up the reins of government than I was obliged to resist the first attack of Sauckel, who demanded the dispatch of hundreds of thousands of French workers to Germany.

My reason for assuming this terrible responsibility at perhaps the most tragic hour of our history is clear.

I owed a great debt to my country. From the most modest origins I had mounted the ladder of power and achievement to its top rung. Did I have the right, when France lay prostrate, to evade the responsibility of serving and attempting to save her? Had I done this I should have been nothing more than a politician anxious above all to serve his personal interests and maintain his reputation before the electorate. I should not have followed the dictates of my heart. In accepting this grave responsibility I followed the commands of my conscience.

Those who persecute me to-day can have only one justification: that they did not know the truth and were ignorant of the facts which I have now presented.

Everything militated against the success of my mission at

that time, but to-day the balance sheet must be in my favour. Truth and justice are two inseparable terms. When they are dissociated the possibility of a judicial crime emerges. I am not fearful of political passion; the only thing of which I am afraid is a lie.

All that I ask is that I shall be allowed to defend myself. If I am permitted to do so it will be clear that I was guilty of no crime. I was the willing victim of a great sacrifice.

I do not ask for mercy. I face with pride the persecution directed against me. I am confident that Frenchmen will not convict me for the sole reason that I loved my country too much.

CHAPTER 10

THE PERSECUTED: JEWS, COMMUNISTS, AND FREEMASONS

THE laws regulating the situation of the Jews were signed in 1940 by the Ministers of Justice and of the Interior. I took no part in their drafting and sponsoring. They were the cruellest burden which the conqueror obliged us to bear. There is no need to point out that for Hitler the Jewish question was the core of everything. Whereas, before the war, anti-semitism was a relatively rare phenomenon in France, the mania of a handful of groups and publicists, in Germany, on the contrary, it was an official doctrine, with its apologists, a bureaucracy to enforce it and, most terrible of all, its executioners. The Jews had to flee from Germany and tens of thousands of them found refuge in France. Here the German army and police found them when our country, as a consequence of its defeat, was no longer in a position to protect them.

The Government's primary duty was to protect French Jews. The law of 1940, which I had no part in formulating, was the lesser of the two evils. It was a Jewish red herring drawn across the trail of the German police and, paradoxical though it may seem, a measure which by gaining time was to prove most helpful to the French Jews. By vaunting to the Germans that our services were going to take action against the French Jews, we dissuaded the Germans from taking action which would have been a thousand times more harsh.

I cannot equitably be held responsible for these laws passed at a time when my influence with the Marshal was virtually nil (I need not again recall that I was arrested on 13 December) and my power over the other ministers to all practical purposes non-existent. Had I been responsible for

them the Marshal and his ministers had only to abrogate
them after my ejection from office. They did nothing of the
sort, for the very good reason that I was not directly or indirectly the author of the laws of 1940.

When I returned to power I faced a situation which required energetic action and vital decisions. I explained in
detail to the examining magistrate what actually took place.
He asked me why I attached to my personal office the Commissariat for Jewish Affairs. I took this step precisely in
order to place this Commissariat under my personal authority. In the intervening years since 1940 the persecution
of the Jews had grown steadily worse. A special anti-Jewish
police, which was set up by the Darlan Government, consisted
almost exclusively of personnel drawn from the extreme
collaborationist parties, such as the P.P.F., who directly followed the orders of the German police. Towards the end of
April 1942 I suppressed this anti-Jewish police. This was only
a few days after my return to office, and I took this action
in the face of the most vigorous protest and threats of the German services, of Darquier de Pellepoix and other French collaborationist parties. A violent Press campaign was launched
against me and against M. Bousquet, the Secretary-General
of the police, by certain picked newspapers which were in the
pay of the occupying power. Bousquet was summoned to
General Oberg and had to submit to a violent 'dressing-
down'.

Next I rejected without hesitation a series of proposed
bills which would have made the condition of the Jews even
more tragic than it already was and I took this action in the
face of, once more, violent attack, originating with the same
persons, the same services, and the same newspapers as had
attacked me previously.

Some of these measures were the following:

One was aimed at such property as remained to the Jews
by providing for a re-examination of the sale of their property previously effected, in the sense that this examination

would cover a period preceding the enactment of the law providing for the sale of Jewish goods.

A second had for its object the hastening of the liquidation of property held in common by a husband and wife in cases where a woman was married to a Jew. The process was to be hurried by the appointment of an expert, who would arbitrarily determine the sum to which the wife was entitled.

A third aimed to suppress the provision whereby a person acquiring Jewish property could not sell it before the expiration of a two-year period: the purpose of this was to speed-up the sale of sequestrated Jewish goods.

Another measure which I indignantly rejected would have imposed penalties on those who were only partly Jewish.

I cite these, among many examples, to show that my opposition to the penalising of the Jewish community was consistent. This was my negative action. In a positive sense I did everything in my power to spare the Jews and save them from the cruel measures imposed by our conquerors. In truth, my policy was a consistent, tenacious, and unrelenting opposition to the German policy.

A further proof of the effectiveness of my opposition is contained in the articles and statements which Darquier de Pellepoix inspired or gave to certain sheets such as *Le Pilori* or *Je suis partout*. He complained bitterly of my attitude and stated specifically that I was blocking by every possible means his anti-Jewish activity.

Another specific example of my attitude was my uncompromising opposition to the effort of the Germans and of the Commissariat for Jewish Affairs to oblige Jews to wear a yellow star while in the Southern Zone. The Germans were in occupation of the Southern Zone at this time and they were insistent that identity and food cards carried by persons of the Jewish religion should be stamped 'Jew.' I decided to stand my ground with regard to the yellow star and to concede if necessary the stamping of the card, because the French authorities, with whom the Jews would have to deal in these fields, would ignore the stamp and it would permit the Jews to be rescued from shipment to Germany. By identifying them in this way, the French local authorities could connive at delivering them from this exile, and concomitantly I issued the most categorical orders to all authorities to withdraw the Jews whenever possible from the list of those tagged for work in the Reich. As a consequence of this step, only at the very last minute were they seized for work, and then under the Todt organisation, and this was an infinitesimal number.

Once more, when later in 1944 the Germans decided to confiscate Jewish property in the Southern Zone, allegedly in apartments not then inhabited, for distribution to the victims of bombardments in France and also in Germany, I protested immediately and vigorously. I was obliged not to resist a limited application of this order, but I forced the confiscating authorities to proceed in an orderly manner, to make an inventory of the goods seized, and to deposit these lists with the French authorities, so that the Jewish owners would have a basis for the recovery of their property at a later date.

With this purpose I issued an order to the Secretary-General of the Police and every measure was taken to enforce my order. Happily, because of the military developments this confiscation was not put into effect. Moreover, I made every effort with the German authorities to persuade them to turn over confiscated Jewish goods to the 'Domaines' (a special office of the French State which acts as a custodian of seized properties pending their legal disposal to new owners) instead of to the Commissariat for Jewish Affairs. To accomplish this I formulated and submitted to the Germans a draft ordinance, but they refused to hear of it.

I cite some of these activities, and this is only a very incomplete list, just to prove that my policy was far from being 'the German one' with which I am charged in the Accusation. This charge was, of course, trumped up in my absence. I was not given an opportunity to defend myself and the charge is worded in such a way as to make me appear as having voluntarily given ground to the Germans in the field in which they were the most merciless and harsh.

The real fact is that it was in this field that I had one of my greatest struggles with the Germans and their French accomplices. I fought ceaselessly against their acts of direct cruelty, acts which no simple hostility to the Jews could possibly justify. I do not exaggerate when I say that I was able to save the lives of thousands of French Jews. Very often I fought in vain to obtain the release of Jews who were my personal friends, because the Germans took a sadistic pleasure in refusing me their release. In addition, I sought by hook or by crook to discover where the Jews were being sent. The reply of the Germans was invariably 'to Poland, where we are creating a Jewish State'. I challenged this statement when I could because my information was that the Jews were being sent to Poland indeed, but only to work under hopeless conditions, to suffer and to die.

It is a cruel and unfair charge to suggest that I could have any sympathy for, and much less sponsor, a policy which would discriminate against fellow human beings who, in coming into the world, could not choose their race or their religion. Frequently, in my political career, I was singled out as a Jew. Never once, during many long years, did Maurras fail, when he spoke of me, to describe me as a Jew or to add the fantastic statement that my wife was a Portuguese Jewess. I was even questioned about this during my electoral campaign and I replied that, although my wife and I were of Auvergnat origin, 'had I been a Jew it would not have been my fault; also, had I been one, I should not have been ashamed of my origin'.

To this reminiscence of my political career I may be permitted to add the comment that throughout my political experience I consistently had Jewish collaborators, some of whom have had very successful careers and who are very well known.

I merely recite these details to demonstrate that I never lived in an anti-semitic atmosphere.

One more illustration of my successful opposition to the Germans comes to my mind. Had I not intervened this time the consequences would have been most tragic for all naturalised Jews. In 1943 the Germans, that is, all the competent German services, together with the Commissariat for Jewish Affairs, tried to force me to sign a law which would have deprived all naturalised Jews of their French nationality. This law would have carried with it the obligation to publish in the *Journal Officiel* the names and addresses of persons thus deprived of French nationality. The purpose of this provision was clear: it was to simplify the task of the German police, who would have proceeded immediately, had this provision gone into effect, to arrest and deport all these unfortunate people.

I stood my ground despite every form of pressure and despite the open threats of the German authorities. I was attacked, denounced, and insulted by the hireling Press, but I refused to budge. In order to resist and delay action I engaged in every subterfuge. In the long run I wore down the Germans, although they never forgave me for this and continued to make capital out of it. This was seized upon by Doriot, who sought, by frequently citing this example of my obstinacy, to prove to the Germans that they could not count upon me and that I ought to be forced to resign.

In a word, I can say without reservation that I did everything in my power to prevent the sadistic brutality of this German policy just as I held in scorn those few Frenchmen who followed or encouraged it.

I well remember meeting a young German captain, a member of one of the anti-Jewish services, whose fanaticism bordered on frenzy. I took great pains to express to the higher German authorities my surprise that such a creature should have been sent to France on such a mission. He was recalled, but those who came after him, although perhaps milder in appearance, were, in fact, nearly as fanatical.

The Jewish people, who are mourning their dead, have every right to complain of the fanatical measures of which they were the victims and to criticise the helplessness of the French Government which, in so many instances, failed to extricate them from their torture by the Germans. But should they not, if only in the name of truth, look the facts squarely in the face when they are brought to light, as they now can be, and have the good grace to admit that I did everything in my power to help them? I am prepared to admit that my power was limited, but this I can say with pride, my will to help them never failed. I say with all humility: there are tens of thousands of Jewish people in France who owe to me their liberty and their lives.

The Accusation sets much store by the fact that the French police, working with the Gestapo, arrested more than 22,000 people in one night. In order to reply effectively I should have to have access to the documents. I should have to be able to consult with certain high officials, notably the Prefect of Police. But from my cell this is impossible, and so I shall have to draw on my memory in order to refute this charge with facts and to justify my continued presence in the Government.

One day in July 1942, if I am not mistaken, I received a call from a certain Colonel Knochen. The object of his visit was to notify me that the German Government had decided to deport every Jewish man, woman, and child then living in France. No distinction was made between Jews of French nationality and others. The Prefect of Police had already been notified by the German authorities of their decision in this matter.

I protested vigorously and hurried to the German Ambassador, who said that he was helpless. The information had already been given to the Paris Press. The ubiquitous Darquier de Pellepoix had already issued a statement. I interceded with General Oberg and, on returning to Vichy, conferred with M. Bousquet. General Oberg's position was made painfully clear to me.

'The trains are ready,' he said. 'They have to be filled at any price. The Jewish problem has no frontiers for us. The police must help us or we shall do the arresting without any distinction between French Jews and others.'

I had to make a rapid decision and determine, for want of anything better, to take every step possible to defend French nationals. As a consequence, if the French police were obliged to intervene in this sorry situation, it was under threat; specifically under the menace of the dark shadow which hung over our fellow-citizens of the Jewish faith.

Upon my return to Vichy I conferred also with M. Rochat, who at once notified the foreign Ambassadors and Ministers and begged them to intervene, without delay, with the German authorities to save their nationals of the Jewish faith then resident in France. I recall that the Spanish and Turkish Ambassadors took immediate action, and so did the Roumanian and Hungarian Ministers. I happened to know that the Spanish Ambassador intervened, with success.

General Oberg, on this occasion, repeated to me once again that it was the intention of the German Government to set up a Jewish State in the East, carved out of Polish territory.

I informed the Marshal of these events and narrated the developments to the Council of Ministers. The Marshal recorded his opinion that we had done everything which possibly could be done under the circumstances.

I also informed the Papal Nuncio of these events and I cooperated with Bousquet to place every difficulty in the way of a successful execution of this decision, but the Germans continued to threaten us with the deportation of the French Jews. I also summoned all the Prefects and explained to them what had taken place. Moreover, in the face of German opposition I managed to have excepted from this measure all foreign Jews married to French nationals and all Jews who had rendered distinguished services to France. Oberg protested violently and claimed that his action was taken in conformity with Article 3 of the Armistice Convention. I was the recipient of an official letter from the German Embassy confirming this viewpoint. Despite the strenuous objection of the German authorities all the exceptions which I had formulated were maintained. Thus, once more, I had shown what I was able to do to defend the Jews of French nationality and to save them. I reject any responsibility for the inhuman and unjust measures of which Jews of foreign extraction were the victims. I employed every measure at my command in an effort to save them. For example, I induced the Germans not to separate children from their parents. I did all that I could, considering the fact that my first duty was to my fellow-countrymen of Jewish extraction, whose interests I could not sacrifice. The right of asylum was not respected in this case. How could it have been otherwise in a country which was occupied by the German army? How could the Jews have been better protected in a country where the Gestapo ran riot?

I did everything in my power to assist the immigration of Jews singly or in groups to foreign countries. Thousands were permitted to cross the Southern Zone to Switzerland, Spain, and Portugal. I strove to arrange through negotiation the departure of 5,000 Jewish children to the United States or to Switzerland, but here again I met with a brutal refusal on the part of the Germans, who claimed that the arrival of these children in the aforementioned countries would furnish a pretext for anti-German demonstrations.

These, in brief, are the facts; these were my acts. Taken together they constitute a clear reply to the Act of Accusation formulated against me in connection with the measures taken by the Germans against the Jews. I should willingly agree to stand in judgment before French Jews on this charge. Surely they, better than others without any doubt, must understand to-day what would have happened to them had I not been there to defend their interests.

Everyone knew that I actively disapproved the measures taken against the secret societies. These measures were taken under the authority of a law drafted in 1940 without my knowledge and, much less, my approval. It was quite clear that the anti-masonic law was inspired by reactionary and clerical circles with which I was not identified, and a large percentage of my difficulties with the Marshal and his entourage may be attributed to our sharp difference of views on this subject. Marshal Pétain sincerely believed that freemasonry was at the root of most of our misfortunes and he looked upon its members as public malefactors. I did not conceal my opinion that many Freemasons in public life set an example of honour and integrity which could well be followed by the representatives of other parties. There were, of course, exceptions which proved the rule. But it was absurd, ridiculous, and dishonest besides to question the patriotism of all the members of the secret societies. As my record was clear in this respect (I never joined a secret society) I could speak freely to the Marshal, without any fear of being accused of acting for a group as a member and a partisan. All the more easily could I criticise and disapprove, as I did on every occasion, the absurd and wicked law of 1940 and the action which was taken in its name. I do not know to what extent the Germans were responsible for inspiring this law, but I do know that I spoke to them time after time without mincing words and told them how useless, unjust, and stupid these laws were.

The anti-masonic laws barred those who had been members of these secret societies from public office; their names had to be published in the *Journal Officiel,* thereby exposing them to persecution. All public officials had to sign a statement indicating whether or not they had ever belonged to the secret societies. False statements were punished with heavy penalties and the names of those guilty of making false statements were published in the *Journal Officiel.*

I was particularly outraged when I learned that M. Alphonse Richard, a Judge of the Court of Appeal, had been obliged to retire because he was accused of having served as an officer of a masonic lodge. Judge Richard, the terror of dishonest profiteers, was one of the most honourable and distinguished magistrates who ever graced our bench. At an earlier date he had been one of my immediate collaborators.

When I heard of the action which had been taken against him I went to see him at once and apologised to him for this ludicrous and odious miscarriage of ordinary justice. The crazy men who were responsible for tragic absurdities such as these could not get it through their dull heads that they were guilty of the worst offences against the honour and dignity of France. The anti-masonic services went so far on this road that they tried to concoct a case, based on a plain forgery, against M. Marchandeau, Mayor of Reims. M. Marchandeau was able to refute their charge with scorn.

Had I been in a position to do so I should have annulled all these laws and put an end to this crying scandal. But the Germans were ever present and in this particular field the Marshal and his personal entourage were passionately involved in the persecution of the masons. All I could hope to do was to limit the effect of these measures and hamper the execution of them to the full extent of my ability. For example, as a consequence of the cases which I have cited above, I was able to issue an order to the effect that there should be no further publication of names in the *Journal Officiel* without previous notice to the Ministry of Justice. This measure sometimes enabled me to delay action, at other times to prevent action entirely.

Then the Commission under M. Reclus was created, and the affair developed into a running battle between the fanatics of the anti-masonic services and myself. Almost invariably they resorted to the Germans in order to attempt to intimidate me. Or, if it was not the Germans, they went to certain individuals in the immediate entourage of the Marshal.

I wish to cite one specific case to illustrate how they operated. I had charged Colonel Bernon, a splendid officer and administrator, to direct a special service responsible for reviewing the cases of persons who were administratively interned. He had forgotten entirely that long before, in

1911, he had joined a small masonic lodge at Saint Germain en Laye. The anti-masonic services dug out this obscure fact and brought it to the attention of the Marshal, or at least one of his immediate collaborators. A clash between the Marshal and myself followed and as a result of this case I obtained a further relaxing of the law in the sense that henceforth even persons accused of making a false declaration were permitted to bring their case to the attention of the Commission, presided over by M. Reclus. This was the limit, however, to which I was able to go in view of the stubborn opposition of the Marshal. But I never missed an occasion to weaken the effect of the law and to promote a liberal interpretation of it.

Under these circumstances is it equitable to hold me responsible for these measures? It seems to me that the prosecution has completely failed to prove its case.

If I could be judged by a jury of Freemasons, and were it possible to inform them fully of the real circumstances, I have no doubt that they would not only absolve me but would congratulate me on the services which I rendered as a member of the Government in preventing by every means possible the execution of this grotesque legislation of which they were the intended victims.

In reply to this charge it should suffice to repeat the questions which were put to me by the pre-trial judge, and my replies, which I shall develop at greater length when my trial takes place.

I never sponsored any legislation directed against the Communists. The Government which preceded that of 10 July 1940 had deported Communists to Africa. I did not. I struck from the draft law having to do with court martials the word 'Communist'. I brought about the release of thousands of members of this party from concentration camps. I gave specific instructions to Prefects and police always to distinguish sharply between the organised resistance, which they were specifically forbidden to impede, and the terrorist bands guilty of criminal activities.

The State Prosecutor takes the view that a distinction of this sort was impossible to make, but I think that it should be recorded here that the distinction *was* made and that many officials of my Government paid with their freedom and their lives for the liberalism which they displayed towards the legitimate resistance forces. Finally, the Germans in concert with the Marshal obliged me to dismiss Bousquet, who was held responsible for this policy of liberalism, and to substitute Darnand in his place. From that moment the methods of the Gestapo prevailed where before there had been a courageous and humane handling of this problem. All control was taken from me and the most I could do was to intervene whenever possible in order to limit the abuses of which Darnand's Militia was guilty. Once again, had I then left office, the road would have been clear for an unrestrained persecution by fanatics who would have had eight long months in which to crucify the French people, without any control whatsoever or any check on their power. By staying in office I was able to maintain in their functions —and this despite the most ferocious German pressure—the Prefect of Police in Paris and the normal cadres in the provinces, which served as shields and barriers to the lust of the Germans, Darnand's Militia, and the collaborationists for the blood of their fellow-countrymen.

It is, therefore, profoundly unjust to hold me responsible for the terror which I did everything in my power to thwart with the feeble means at my command.

I reject this accusation with indignation. My only comment is that it would have been cowardly for me to abandon my post in this critical hour and thereby expose the French people to a reign of terror which, measured in terms of human suffering and chaos, would have been without parallel in Western Europe. No; there was no choice for me. Every loyal and humane consideration required me to remain at my post at that critical time when the harshness and inhumanity of the Germans was increasing in proportion as they suffered military defeat and underwent more and more severe bombardments. I could have taken the coward's way and abandoned my country to their barbaric ferocity. Without the presence of a government to hold the breach, they would have wasted our country in that final stage and decimated its people.

The 'Greek Chorus' of the hireling Press shrieked all this time for my removal from office because of my refusal to take my hands off the brake. It screamed for a Government to be composed of Doriot, Déat, and Darnand. What further proof is needed of the necessity for me to remain at my post?

It is my duty to record without exaggeration the simple fact that by remaining in office I saved many French lives. I have already had occasion to speak before the High Court of Justice concerning the assassination of M. Mandel and M. Jean Zay. The following summary may, I believe, be deemed opportune.

The German Ambassador informed me one day of his Government's decision to have Paul Reynaud, Léon Blum, and George Mandel—who had been deported to Germany and interned there—transferred to French authority that they might be shot in reprisal for the death sentence of Admiral Derrien, pronounced by the Council of War at Algiers. Against this, I spontaneously and vigorously protested and I vetoed the German proposal, which I qualified as odious and unjust. MM. Blum, Reynaud, and Mandel could not in any way be held responsible for a sentence issued in Algiers. Knowing, however, through this communication, that their lives might be in danger, I hastened to inform the Committee of Algiers that I had received it, and that my response had been a clear and stern negative.

I saw Señor de Lequerica, the Spanish Ambassador, and gave him a memorandum to this effect, the contents of which he promised to make known to the Algiers Committee. I informed Herr Abetz of my initiative and told him that Señor de Lequerica had accepted the mission thus entrusted to him.

I also let the Cabinet Council know all that had happened and communicated to the ministers the text of the Lequerica memorandum; a copy of this will be found in the archives of the Foreign Affairs Department. Shortly thereafter, Señor de Lequerica informed me that the Algiers Committee had thanked the Spanish Government for its communication. As time passed, I was led to believe that my firm response to this odious proposal, transmitted directly by the German Ambassador to his Government, had forestalled this catastrophe, and I hoped to hear nothing more about it.

Not long after, however, at a date I cannot exactly specify, on returning to Vichy after one of my frequent trips to Paris, I received a telephone call from M. de Brinon, informing me of the decease of M. Mandel. He could give me no further detail than that it had occurred in France. I ordered him to summon immediately his informer, M. Knipping, who, questioned in an imperative manner, pleaded total ignorance of the circumstances but promised as soon as possible to communicate the results of the investigation I asked him to conduct.

I then summoned Darnand to my office and received confirmation of M. Mandel's death. As I had been led to believe that he was in Germany, I asked Darnand how he had learned of his death. He then explained that on the previous day the German police had transferred George Mandel to his own services in Paris and that consequently he must have died in France. I pressed him with questions he seemed incapable of answering, telling me that he had received news of his death but knew nothing of the circumstances attending it, and was also entirely ignorant of how M. Mandel came to be transferred to his services. 'Knipping alone will be able to inform you of that,' said he. I phoned directly to M. de Brinon in Paris. Knipping was in his office. According to him, M. Mandel had been transferred the day before, placed in M. Baillet's custody, and interned at La Santé prison whence, next day, he was expedited to the Château des Brosses, near Vichy, for internment. During the trip the car in which he had been placed was attacked and, during the skirmish, M. Mandel was killed. I protested with violence and indignation. I asked why I had not immediately been informed of the transfer of M. Mandel, why M. Baillet had not told me that he had been interned at the Santé prison, and why he had been transferred to the Château des Brosses. I did not conceal my opinion as to the real cause of his death.

I had been George Mandel's friend for thirty years. I had backed him when, for the first time, he became a Cabinet member. He, in turn, had backed me to enter the Clemenceau Government, which I was unable to do, as the Socialist Party, of which I was then a member, had refused to collaborate with M. Clemenceau. Our friendship had strengthened as the years went by and remained firm even when we did not agree on certain political points. If he were alive to-day I know that he would defend me. His death was a great shock —all the more tragic because for a time I thought I had saved his life.

After Mandel's assassination I sent out an order to Darnand and to Knipping instructing them to refuse the transfer of Léon Blum and Paul Reynaud, or that of any other French political personality in the custody of the Germans. I instructed them to call immediately to my attention any communication with regard to such a matter, and filed another protest with the German Ambassador against these inhuman and barbaric methods.

I informed the Cabinet of my indignation, and ordered the Ministry of Justice to open an investigation to determine the circumstances surrounding M. Mandel's death and to indict all those who were responsible. M. Gabolde had already taken certain steps and he promised to follow this case with the utmost care. The investigation had not been completed when I was deported to Germany on 17 August 1944.

The Germans had also demanded the arrest of hostages from among the families of various members of the Algiers Committee. These persons had been detained only a few days when the Germans came to me and asked, as they had done in the case of Blum, Reynaud, and Mandel, that they be shot. Backed by articles which had appeared in certain Paris newspapers, they requested the immediate execution of these persons as reprisal for the execution of certain collaborationists in Northern Africa. I protested violently against these methods, saying: 'They may be in good odor in your country but they are not admissible in ours.' I added bluntly: 'I have no blood on my hands and I consider your proposal a personal and a grave offence.'

When I returned to power in April 1942 I was able to persuade the Germans to take no more hostages. They solemnly promised this and for more than two years they refrained from making such demands, as odious as they were shameful. This did not prevent them from resorting to bloody reprisals in spite of the indignant protests which were filed by the French Government, but the odious method of taking hostages was abandoned for two years.

They also promised not to hamper the refugees from Alsace and Lorraine who were in the Southern Zone when it was invaded in November 1942, and also not to arrest any of the 80,000 prisoners who had escaped from Germany and who had taken refuge in the Southern Zone. They kept these promises.

As the American troops were approaching Paris I feared that the Germans might resort to reprisals against the political prisoners then detained in French prisons, or that they might deport them to Germany. Consequently, I told Baillet to open the gates of all the prisons. I could not, of course, have given such an order at an earlier date, as the Germans might have used this as a pretext to resort to much more severe measures. The French prisons had been placed under Darnand's control and under the supervision of Baillet. I had known Baillet's father very well. He had been the Police Commissioner at Pantin and Noisy-le-Sec when I was the representative of these towns in Congress. M. Baillet's father was an official who commanded the esteem of his chiefs and of the population of his district. I hoped that the son had inherited his father's qualities.

I was able to obtain numerous measures of clemency with regard to the Alsatians and the Bretons who had been sentenced to death by the Germans. My assistants can produce the files relating to thousands of people on whose behalf I interceded.

One day I received the visit of Brun, who was the Prefect of Clermond-Ferrand and who had come to inform me that Marchadier, a Communist leader, had been sentenced to death. I was able to prevent this execution by the Germans. I believe that M. Marchadier is to-day the Mayor of Clermond-Ferrand. May I now be permitted to ask how many members of the present government in France would have escaped with their lives had I deserted my post at a time when the Germans and their friends were prepared to vent their spleen in criminal excesses without let or hindrance?

It is paradoxical to accuse me of responsibility for acts of cruelty which every reasonable and honest man knows I did everything in my power to prevent.

When the Accusation holds me responsible for the persecution of the Communists, it reveals total ignorance of my character and of my deeds.

I have, all my life, been the sworn enemy of violence. I have always been a peace-loving man. Peace has been my ideal, and history shows the persecution of an ideal merely serves to affirm and strengthen it. Prisons, the guillotine, and the firing-squad have made great martyrs; they have never killed an ideal.

CHAPTER 11

GERMAN DEMANDS FOR LABOUR

ACCORDING to the State Prosecution I would have sent French workers to Germany as a voluntary and spontaneous gesture, assisting Hitler in this fashion instead of giving armed assistance. This charge is so very grave that, at the close of my discussion, I shall reply to it clearly and unequivocally.

I have said elsewhere that in March 1942 Goering told me: 'Do not under any circumstance enter the Government; it is both too early and much too late. We shall be obliged, henceforth, to treat France far more harshly.' I meditated on these words in debating what my duty was. I concluded that my duty could in no event be to follow the advice of Goering.

As against my selfish personal interest I preferred the rocky road of sacrifice in the interest of my country; I ought to have received the gratitude of my fellow-countrymen for this choice. Instead, I am the victim of injustice. This is due in part to ignorance of the historical facts of that time. I fully realise this and I shall make it my aim to substitute for this ignorance a knowledge of the truth, which will throw light on my action and show that in this main crisis, as in all the crises during the course of the Occupation, I served my country faithfully and with all the strength and devotion I could command.

In my deposition in the Pétain case I reviewed at some length the situation imposed upon our country by the Armistice Convention. The country was sliced into bits. The Nord and Pas-de-Calais departments were administratively attached to Brussels. There was a line which might not be traversed, called the 'North to East line'. It cut off the area situated to the north of this line, from the mouth of the Somme to the Swiss frontier. Then, there was the line of demarcation between the Occupied and Free Zones, not to speak of Alsace and Lorraine, which were annexed outright by Germany. There was also the provision whereby neither merchandise nor specie might cross the line of demarcation without the complete approval of the German authorities— this meant, in fact, the gradual strangling of the Southern Zone, which had neither bread, meat, nor sugar with which to eke out an existence. Moreover, and these prohibitions applied to both zones, we were reduced to a total of three million tons of coal when 39½ millions represented our minimum needs, to a considerable reduction of our steel, and to virtually no lubricating oils, no petrol, no rubber, no minerals, many of which were essential and which used to come to us from abroad. In addition, the blockade deprived us of foodstuffs and raw materials.

This was the doleful situation with which we were faced as a consequence of the Armistice. In October 1940 over one million Frenchmen were unemployed. Two million of our fellow-countrymen were prisoners in Germany.

Large segments of the population from the North and the East had emigrated to the South, where they were joined by a later influx of refugees from the departments in the centre of France, which had been occupied by the German armies.

In an effort to bring some order out of chaos the first and most urgent measure seemed to be to provide for a return of as many people as possible to their homes. This proceeded normally enough despite the almost total lack of transportation. North of the 'North to East line' the Germans were setting up gigantic airfields, such as the one immediately to the north of Vouziers, and German farmers were pouring into this region to claim the lands deserted by the original French owners. These owners could not obtain passes to return home and were systematically refused permission by the Germans. This was the prevailing situation in the Meurthe-et-Moselle, the Meuse, the Vosges, the Ardennes, the Aisne departments, and even in some parts of the Somme department. The most urgent necessity, if we could not recover our farmlands at once, was to regain at least the immediate control of our coal mines in the Meurthe-et-Moselle and the Ardennes. The first step in this direction was the permission extended in October 1940 to the workmen of the Meuse Valley between Sedan and Givet to return to their homes. By the end of November all these workmen had returned.

In February 1941 the number of unemployed had been reduced to a figure slightly under the normal total in times of plenty and peace. Over a million prisoners had been liberated from the Stalags in France before they could be sent with two million more to Germany in the summer of 1940. Of the two million sent to Germany, all veterans of the war of 1914-1918 and all fathers of four children or more had been freed and the process of freeing other categories of prisoners had begun. Of course, many of those freed lived under the constant threat of being returned to Germany because they were merely on leave from captivity. This, in a few brief words, describes the tragic situation of our country at that time.

The first move of the Germans to obtain manpower in France to replace in the German factories young Germans who had been conscripted occurred in April 1941. At this time they made their first appeal for volunteers, accompanied by an intensive propaganda showing the attractions of work in Germany, notably the high salaries. They founded apprentice schools, the most important of which was located at the arsenal of Puteaux. Moreover, to further their campaign they agreed in May 1941 to a uniform rise in French salaries of one franc for each working-hour. German services were set up to recruit French workers in the Occupied Zone. The French Government did not authorize the functioning of these services in the Southern Zone. Volunteer workers were given one-year contracts which could be extended by the Germans for one more year. It is difficult to estimate the number of workers who left for Germany before May 1942 but the total was around 150,000.

In May 1942 Gauleiter Sauckel approached the French Government for the first time to notify us that the number of volunteers was far from sufficient and that a total of 250,000 would have to be reached before the end of July of that year. He stated that the Government could have the choice between stimulating the departure of volunteer workers and a draft which would be imposed by the German authorities, the workers to be drawn from among the re-patriated prisoners. If, for the sake of discussion, the million prisoners liberated in France in the summer of 1940 are left out of account, the total number of prisoners on leave from captivity then amounted to about 600,000 men. These 600,000 men were the intended victims of Sauckel, who in-timated, moreover, that if we did not produce the workers he would see that we were denied vital shipments of coal and other combustibles and lubricants, thus upsetting our eco-nomic machinery and swelling the ranks of unemployed, whom he would immediately draft for his purposes.

Until this first visit of Sauckel I had not realised how desperate our situation could be. I realised then that in the guise of a volunteer migration to Germany was hidden a plan for deporting huge numbers of French workers in mass. We were powerless to avoid this humiliation and sacrifice, which was obviously to be demanded of us.

The United States had not as yet actively entered the war in Europe. The landing in North Africa was yet to come. Resistance was not organised in France, and the twenty million French workers in field and factory were then an easy prey for Sauckel.

As soon as I realised the full import of Sauckel's designs I protested vigorously. I pointed out that we were not obliged under the Armistice Convention to take this step. I empha-sised that this measure spelled the doom for any possibility of understanding and reconciliation between our two coun-tries. I said, and I repeated, everything that any Frenchman would have expected me to say under these circumstances, and in a tone which suited the occasion.

The conversation with Sauckel was violent throughout and lasted several hours. I was so deeply moved and so exhausted that I fainted in the presence of Sauckel and our conversation had to be interrupted. Isn't this very far from the 'willing and spontaneous collaboration' with Germany, of which I am accused by the State Prosecutor? What else could I do? The Wehrmacht occupied France and Sauckel had every means of enforcing his decision. There could be no doubt of his determination to carry his decision through to the bitter end. He was determined to have these French workers, even if it required the use of force.

It was at this point that I decided to link the question of workers for Germany with the return of prisoners from the Reich. I suggested to Sauckel that in compensation for the departure of workers we should receive an equal number of liberated prisoners. Sauckel sneered cynically: 'You know very well that since General Giraud's escape Hitler has decided not to liberate any more French prisoners.' I replied that it was quite impossible for the French Government to give support even in the slightest degree to the German plan to draft workers for Germany—which, in fact, we had no means of preventing—unless the German Government were at least to admit in principle that we ought to receive compensation in the form of liberated French prisoners.

I was so emphatic in this respect that Sauckel telephoned Hitler, and on the following day he promised me that if 150,000 industrial workers should leave for Germany, 50,000 French agricultural workers would be liberated from the prison camps. 'We cannot possibly admit an exchange on an equal basis,' he said, 'because these French prisoners are already working in Germany and, in addition to losing control of them, we shall lose the benefit of their work.'

I struggled to obtain better terms but it was impossible and I decided that the return of 50,000 Frenchmen was better than nothing at all. I had used every kind of argument and I had achieved some result. I was convinced that no better terms could be obtained at that time. I then had to drain the cup to its bitter dregs and to make the appeal which has been quoted.

My purpose was to obtain volunteers in order to stop the Germans from drafting French workers. I could not help recalling during my conversations with Sauckel the warning which Goering had given me. I had no choice, but had to risk the seemingly legitimate wrath of multitudes of my fellow-countrymen, to whom I could not reveal the real facts. But I knew that certain phrases publicly pronounced by me would enable me to save them from further cruel wrongs at the hands of the Germans.

The whole purpose of my policy at this point was to create an atmosphere of artificial confidence among the German representatives whom I wished to convince that we were doing our best. I had to persuade them that my good-will was assured and that we had reached the limit of our concessions. I preferred to risk unpopularity rather than to expose my country to further tragic tribulations. The return of hundreds of thousands of prisoners, too, was better than the hell of the prison camps.

I do not challenge the right of Frenchmen to question the wisdom of this policy. But I am certain that no man of good-will will wish to question my motive or to challenge the results I was able to obtain.

On 22 June 1942 I spoke the words with which the State Prosecutor charges me. But on 3 September, addressing three hundred schoolteachers at Vichy, I pronounced these words: 'I have had to use words which have gone very far, indeed as far as words can go, but I wish you to understand, and I am certain that you do, that I am willing to run every risk and to expose myself to every attack in order to save France to-day.' These words were almost prophetic; they constituted my reply, as long ago as 1942, to the Accusation which is flung in my face to-day.

What other choice had I, confronted as I was by the German threat to seize the major portion of our manpower? It should not be forgotten, too, that Sauckel's move coincided with the transfer to France of S.S. units and the beginning of persecution by the Gestapo. Goering had been right.

In July and August 1942 very few volunteers offered themselves. Sauckel brutally accused the French Government of bad faith in recruiting workers and decided to institute a system of forced labour, applicable to all men and women in all countries administered or occupied by Germany. The needs of Germany in manpower and material were mounting daily. The battle of Stalingrad had just begun.

This decision of Sauckel was communicated to us in a circular of 20 August 1942 which all the newspapers of the Occupied Zone were obliged to publish. The Germans insisted that it should also be published in the Free Zone, but I notified the German censorship authorities that I would not permit this and I cited the terms of the Armistice Convention to uphold my position. Moreover, I immediately informed the German Embassy that I would resign if Sauckel's order were applied to France.

After hours of insistence the German Government gave way and agreed to postpone immediate application of the Sauckel directive. They vigorously upheld, however, Sauckel's declaration that it was inadmissible for the French to stand with their arms crossed doing nothing in a world at war where the people of all countries were mobilised. He pictured with irony the spectacle of Paris, and the other great cities of France, filled to overflowing with people lolling in cafés and cinemas.

I had succeeded in obtaining a delay in the application of the relentless draft of men and women. Every other occupied country had had to accept it, but I could assure an extension of the delay only by publishing a law which seemed to follow the general line of Sauckel's directive, though, in fact, it was full of loopholes.

This was the law of 4 September 1942, which could oblige men between eighteen and sixty and unmarried women between twenty-one and thirty-five to work, away from their place of residence if necessary. Sauckel, after the promulgation of this law, agreed not to apply his directive to France on condition that the number of French workers in Germany reached a total of 250,000.

I then persuaded him to except from the application of the law all repatriated prisoners in the first instance; next, all natives of Alsace and Lorraine who had found refuge in France, then the fathers of three children, and finally all women. Moreover, he agreed that the French police would not be used.

This gives the background of the law of 4 September 1942. It might be described as lip-service to the Germans. Can I be criticised for this law when it is known that no one in France had any intention of applying it and that it enabled France, and France alone, among the occupied countries of Europe, to escape the application of Sauckel's directive? I had learned how to negotiate with the Germans. I had learned that straight refusals achieved nothing except a harsh reaction against us. The only possible way of handling the Germans and of gaining precious time was to draft texts to exhibit to them but which no one had any intention of applying; indeed, my secret instructions to the Prefects rendered these laws inapplicable. The Germans were quick to note our failures. They had every means of forcing us to act and they were determined to use these means. The dispatch of workers to Germany was mostly from the Northern Zone. It began in the Southern Zone only after the German army crossed the demarcation line. There was never a dispatch of workers which was not the direct result of German pressure.

Three months went by. On 2 January 1943 Sauckel returned to the charge. He said he must have another draft of French workers totalling 250,000, of whom 150,000 had to be specialists. He claimed that he had received a direct order from Hitler to carry out this draft at any cost. There was no question this time of a bilateral negotiation. This was a command.

Once more I tried delaying tactics, despite the fact that I was certain this time that the Germans were prepared to go to extreme limits to enforce their will. Through discussion, negotiation, and compromise, I succeeded in wresting from them a promise that in return for more drafts of French workers they would free 50,000 more French prisoners.

I also obtained an agreement that the figure of 250,000 might be reached by converting prisoners held in Germany in the prison camps into workers with adequate salaries and the right of a two-weeks' leave in France. During this draft the French administration intervened only to prevent the most flagrant injustices in the choice of individuals. Most of the drafting took place in factories and there was a public outcry because in many cases older men were drafted while the younger ones were spared. It was in response to this outcry that it was decided to recruit the 1940 and 1941 classes, and the last third of the class of 1939 with the exception of agricultural workers. The French Government could do nothing, powerless as it was, to resist this latest German ultimatum.

By 10 April 1943 a total of 250,000 workers had left, of whom 170,000 came from factories. Eighty thousand were drawn from the three classes called up under the French draft.

Thereupon, the French Government set up the S.T.O., which was, in fact, a special administration created to regulate the draft. The object was to check the more flagrant abuses of the German administrative machinery.

There was a tendency on the part of the Germans to recruit workers largely from the same industrial areas. This resulted in special hardship and the S.T.O. attempted to prevent it. The departures, owing to the slowing-up process of our services, took place at much longer intervals. Taking as their authority our law of 4 September 1942, the French Administration resisted the drafting of specialists and agricultural workers. Finally, the Germans struck back violently. They called up the entire class of 1942, even including agricultural workers. The response to this measure was inevitable. There was a mass flight of young men to the *maquis*.

As a last-minute measure we persuaded the Germans to exempt rail-workers, miners, policemen, prison officials, and other civil servants. We were able to write in the names of tens of thousands of young Frenchmen on the lists of civil servants and thus save them from deportation; rarely have the enlistments in the police and the penitentiary services reached such heights!

By 30 July 1943, 170,000 men had left under this draft and I decided that the moment had come to inform the German Government that the French Government had decided not to permit any further recruiting. I told the Germans that our circular (curiously enough, the one which was cited against me by the State Prosecutor) was proof of our good faith, but that experience had shown that it was inapplicable, and that I had, in consequence, decided to end the draft.

With this, Sauckel hurried back to Paris to protest and to register new demands. He announced that a million French men and women must be put to work in the French factories in addition to those who were already at work. This million, he said, would allow 500,000 trained workers to be shipped to Germany. He demanded, moreover, heavy drafts for the Todt organisation, which previous to 1944 had, in fact, employed only 20,000. I pointed out to him that these demands were inflated beyond any remote possibility of realisation. My conversation with Sauckel on this occasion was the most painful and trying which I experienced during my entire political career. It took place on 6 August 1943, and I flatly refused to send any further contingents of workers to Germany. Tension with the German authorities reached the breaking-point. Sauckel asked to see Doriot, and on the following day reviewed with him a parade of the P.P.F. along the boulevards of Paris. He criticised me with bitterness. He organised special groups with the mission of recruiting workers, arresting them and denouncing them to the German service entitled the 'Social Peace Organisation'.

These French groups were recruited primarily from the

P.P.F. and were responsible in many departments, notably in the Gironde, for violent incidents. I protested at the German Embassy against the organisation of this special police created by Germans on French territory and consisting of Frenchmen who had the job of enforcing an order of the German authorities. This organisation gave one some idea of what a Doriot regime in France would have been.

At this point the Germans tried a new strategy. They attempted to blackmail the French Government by arresting forty of the highest officials of the Government selected from several ministries. I protested and held my ground, despite this blackmail. I was then ordered to surrender the 30,000 members of the youth camps. This I refused to do. Towards the end of September 1943, Herr Ritter, Sauckel's representative in Paris, was assassinated. I must refer again to the circular of 12 July 1943, of which so much capital has been made. Presumably, it is better understood now that I have placed it in the framework of the real events of that period. This circular was drafted under the direct and imperative pressure of the Germans, but I had no idea of enforcing it and never did enforce it. I defy anyone to cite a single case where measures were taken in France against a doctor who had delivered a false certificate. As soon as this document was circulated I informed the Germans that if it were to be enforced I should halt the recruiting of all workers. The circular was then dropped and never went into effect.

In order to obtain a further delay I succeeded in playing off the Sauckel organisation against that of Speer, the German Minister of Armaments. In January 1944 I brought Sauckel's organisation into opposition with that of Herr Bache, the German Minister of Agriculture. As a result of this rivalry, which I capitalised, I saved the whole peasant and agricultural class from deportation.

Finally, on 16 October 1943, I obtained a delay in all departures, which was extended into 1944.

M. Bichelonne had the primary responsibility in meeting German demands for French workers. My role, with M.

Bichelonne's support, was to argue with Gauleiter Sauckel in order to obtain a scaling down of his demands and a modification of his methods.

It was M. Bichelonne who hit on the idea of setting up an exempt class of French factories, to be known as the 'S' factories, whose workers would not be drafted. He succeeded in placing ten thousand French factories in this category and finally, on 7 October 1943, obtained the German agreement to an exemption from the draft of the innumerable workers whose names had been previously called and who had sought work in these factories. The Germans refused a request that prisoners who had failed to return to Germany at the end of their fifteen days' leave, and who were working in these factories, should be exempted.

In January 1944 the German Government informed us that, apart from any prisoners, 670,000 French workers had been drafted and had gone to Germany, but that this number had fallen to 400,000 because of the failure of workers to return to Germany from France upon the expiration of their leave. As punishment for this failure Sauckel then demanded that a million workers be sent to Germany and that another million be recruited for work in France.

Once more I was obliged to try to gain time. Once more I drafted a paper project, which I had no idea of enforcing, calling up workmen between sixteen and sixty years and unmarried women between eighteen and forty-five. I had also to agree that foreign workers should be dispatched to Germany. The Germans set up a special organisation for the purpose of 'combing' the French labour field, and this organisation had branches even in the smallest towns. The French Government persuaded the Germans to agree to attach French officials to this service in a consultative capacity. The real purpose of this move was to hamper and delay the Germans as much as possible.

We continued also to maintain the immunity of the 'S' factories, placed somewhat under the protection of the Speer organisation, much to the disgust of the Sauckel people, who termed them 'the authorised *maquis*'.

In the first three months of 1944 only 30,000 men left for Germany and these were mostly foreigners. This total was, in fact, less than the number of workers who returned to France during the same period and who remained behind upon the expiration of their leave.

At this point the massive bombardments which France had to undergo after 15 March 1944 created a new and serious problem. The destruction of 'S' factories, which, in agreement with Speer, were exempted from the deportation orders of Sauckel, threw out tens of thousands of workers. They were a ready prey for Sauckel and I felt that I had to gain time by hook or by crook. I did everything in my power to slow down the machinery of deportation. I dodged Sauckel and managed to be out of Paris when he was there. I resorted to every subterfuge to gain vital hours and days.

Finally, came the landing in Normandy. Despite the approach of our liberators the German demand for workers went on and their threats never ceased. I resorted to the stratagem of playing the Germans off against one another. Then, on a date which I cannot check in my prison cell (it must have been about the 10th or 11th of June), I dispatched a confidential telegram to all Prefects, instructing them to refuse any further drafts. This was at a time when the Germans, because of military developments, were becoming daily more jumpy and more harsh. The German manpower services registered a vigorous protest with me. I said that I could not retract an order which was irrevocable and which I had communicated to the German Embassy.

On 17 August I was taken from Paris by force, on an order of the German Government communicated by the German Embassy and enforced by the Gestapo. I then declared that I had to cease to exercise the functions of my office. Following this date, as the Germans withdrew, they conducted raids to obtain fresh manpower, particularly in the east, and the entire population of many towns was deported to Germany for forced labour. The east of France for a few short weeks experienced the methods which the Germans had applied for some years throughout occupied Europe and even in the north of Italy. This was a taste of what France would have suffered had I not negotiated, manœuvred, acted, and spoken as I did to thwart and rein in the aggressive Sauckel and his host of slave-drivers.

In a word, my crime was to have protected several hundreds of thousands of Frenchmen and Frenchwomen, I should write millions, who, had it not been for the activity displayed by my Government, would certainly have been deported to Germany. My further crime was to have obtained the release from German prison camps of 110,000 prisoners, after the day when Hitler issued his categorical order that not a single further French prisoner should be released.

To sum up, the results of my activity in this manpower field were the following: On 5 June 1942, before the American landing in North Africa and the organisation of active resistance in France, I had to face an order of Sauckel to place at the disposal of the German factories the whole body of French workers, women as well as men. Twenty million French workers were employed at the time in the factories and fields of France and there was nothing to prevent the Germans from enslaving them, as they had done in Poland, in Holland, in Czechoslovakia and elsewhere. Between 5 June 1942 and 30 July 1944, 2,060,000 workers were demanded of France. No *quid pro quo* was to have been given for the drafted workers. As a result of my efforts, those of the Government and of the administrative officials, the following was the balance sheet after two years of struggle, specifically on 30 July 1944:

Between 5 June 1942 and 30 July 1944, 341,500 workers left for Germany (this figure does not take into account the tens of thousands who, after obtaining a two-weeks' leave to visit their homes in France, failed to return to Germany).

As against this, 110,000 prisoners returned to France, including 100,000 farmers and peasants and 10,000 disabled men. From 15 April 1943 the fifteen-days' leave privilege was obtained for all former war prisoners. From 16 October 1943 all departures for Germany were suspended except on a direct exchange basis, the total number of workers in Germany having dropped by this time to 400,000. Finally, on 7 June 1944, all departures were halted.

At all times the number of workers sent to Germany was very much less than the number of prisoners returned to France. The total of workers in Germany, including a large number of volunteers, never exceeded 670,000. After 16 October 1943 this number steadily decreased. By the same token, the number of prisoners, which totalled three million when the Armistice was signed, dropped progressively to 1,050,000 by 1943.

All other countries of Europe, Belgium, Holland, Poland, and the rest, suffered manpower drafts totalling fifty to eighty per thousand of the population, women as well as men, while the total for France (excluding, of course, the returned prisoners) never exceeded thirteen per thousand and not a single woman was drafted.

Could there be any more convincing rebuttal of the accusations brought against me? If the figures which I have cited for the other European countries are exact, and they can easily be checked, is there any better justification for the presence of a government in France during the Occupation?

My personal role was consistent in every field. When France was strong and victorious I was her chosen spokesman on many an occasion. I was proud of my role then.

During the Occupation years, and especially in connection with this manpower problem, I was obliged to carry a heavy cross. Is it less patriotic and less noble to suffer for one's country in time of sorrow and stress than to enjoy its triumphs when it is happy and strong?

Was it better to attempt to negotiate with the Germans, to delay their action, to hem them in when possible, or should

I have followed the easy course of letting them track down Frenchmen like beasts of prey? More than two million men were marked down for deportation; less than a third of this number were actually taken. It is perfectly human for the workers who had to suffer one or two years of heartrending exile to bear me ill-will. It is likewise perfectly human for those who were saved from this fate through my efforts to forget the part I played in their escape. But had I not acted as I did a vast army of workers would have been added to the list of deportees, and not a single prisoner of war would have come home.

The figures and the facts speak for me.*

* See Appendix V, text of Sauckel's report to Hitler, dated 9 August 1943, denouncing Laval. This report was found in the German archives in Berlin.

CHAPTER 12

WORDS WHICH I SPOKE

I NOW must dwell for a few moments on the words with which I am reproached. Most of the quotations which are cited in the Accusation are incorrect and in certain instances words are put into my mouth which I never used. For example, I am accused of having said at Compiègne that 'no trumpet will sound for the release of prisoners until the day when German victory is consummated'. I happen to have the printed text of the statements which I made in Compiègne when greeting several thousand war prisoners on their return from Germany. No such words are in the text. When I spoke of the liberation of the great body of our prisoners these were my words:

'How I yearn to be able to say some words which would give hope to our prisoners languishing in the camps! There are still more than 1,200,000 out there and France awaits their return with a wholly natural and legitimate impatience. We need them at home because they are the living strength of our country, but laws of war exist which have unhappy consequences, and one of these laws is that prisoners remain in the hands of their captors until peace is signed. Following the Armistice over 2,000,000 were in the camps. Several hundred thousands have been liberated.'

It is hard for me to understand, in the light of this text, and in view of the grave charges against me, why words which I never uttered should be placed in my mouth. The statements upon which I must stand and on which I can be challenged are those which I made officially and which were officially recorded. For example, there can be no question about the authenticity of my speeches before the National Assembly and over the radio. The same thing cannot be said about statements attributed to me in the Paris Press, which was constantly hostile to me. These texts, as everyone knows, were frequently falsified by the German propaganda services. This was a common practice of German propaganda, which invented statements *ad lib.*, attributing them variously to Joan of Arc, Victor Hugo, Napoleon, and Clemenceau, and filling the newspapers with, and writing on the walls, quotations, many of which could easily be challenged. Time and again I protested to Ambassador Abetz about these practices. I did not publish denials in the Southern Zone because for obvious reasons I was not looking for additional trouble with the German administration. Also, I had enough experience of journalism to understand that the next edition wipes out the one before. I could not possibly have foreseen that these questionable texts would, one day, be seriously discussed before a High Court of Justice.

I turn next to the statement which, above all, is held against me and which is quoted in the prosecution charge as: 'I foresee a German victory.' I have already commented upon this, during the Pétain trial. I had written: 'I believe in a German victory and foresee it.' At the specific direction of the Marshal, who pointed out that as a civilian I was not competent to judge military events, I scratched out the words 'I believe' and, in agreement with him, left in the words 'I foresee.' Monsieur Rochat's testimony removes all shadow of doubt with regard to this. It is regrettable, I am more than ready to admit, that the text was modified at the Marshal's request, because the statement, as first drafted and for the reasons which I have explained, was strictly limited in scope. To say that one looks forward to an event which appears certain adds nothing to the force of one's belief.

To appreciate fully the meaning of my words, the time when they were spoken as well as the circumstances of my return to power must be taken into consideration. I made my statement on 5 June 1942. Germany had then decided to treat France with extreme rigour. My conversation with Goering left no doubt whatever about this fact. I knew, therefore, that

my task, already so heavy, was to become still more difficult.
I had the feeling that if I were able to create an atmosphere
of confidence between the two governments I should be in a
much better position to protect the forty million French
people from the increasing harshness of enemy occupation.
This was the essential mission I had set myself to accomplish.
It seemed to me that in taking sides publicly I should have
better means and more facilities at my disposal in the inevitable and forthcoming negotiations with the Germans. I
never doubted for one second that such words would be held
against me. The first duty of a statesman is never to fear
making himself unpopular when he knows that at this price
only can he make himself really useful to his country. In
any case, this is the principle I had laid down for myself
on entering public life. In all the discussions I had with
Sauckel, which were as numerous as were his exigencies, my
words allowed me to force him to acknowledge that if I refused to comply with his demands it was because the prime
interests of the nation made it impossible for me to accept
them.

One day I told him: 'You behave as though we were vanquished and yet you want us to act as if we were your allies.
You complain of the hostility aroused by your demands.' All
those who attended these arduous negotiations can testify
to-day that each time I argued with him, he was moved to
lessen his pretentions. Yet, never could I have used the tone
I did nor obtained the positive results which to-day are on
record had it not been that my statement of 5 June 1942 gave
me, in his eyes, the authority of a man who has shown himself
to have risen above his fear. The words now held against me
did more than anything else to facilitate my hard task and to
smooth out the many difficulties which I had to settle each
day with the authorities of occupation.

People forget to-day that when I made my statement in
June 1942 the American landing in North Africa had not
yet taken place. The only battle front in Europe, upon which
all eyes were focussed, extended from Finland to the Cau-

casus, and I still thought that a German victory there was probable. To-day, Germany is defeated and my remark may indeed appear unfortunate to those who forget that when my words were uttered they made possible the actions which I had planned and were then essential to the interests of the French people, who were under the heel of the conqueror.

It must also be remembered that there were in Paris, at that very time, certain persons, certain groups of ardent collaborationists, who had gained the ear of the German authorities and who, feeling that they were backed by them, engaged in a fierce campaign against my policies and were endeavouring to get into power.* My statement cut the ground from under their feet and allowed me, as Prime Minister, and Minister of Foreign Affairs, to continue the policy of neutrality which gave me the maximum of independence in the face of the Germans. I spoke, in order not to act. Without my statement, Doriot would have had less difficulty in attaining his ends.

Almost invariably when my words are quoted the end of my sentence is purposely omitted. Referring to the gigantic combats which were taking place in Russia, I said: 'I foresee a German victory, *for without that, Communism will be rampant throughout Europe.*' This prophecy seemed to me to envision the natural order of events. After her collapse, Germany might be led into Communism more easily than into any other kind of regime, on account of the collective life and discipline to which she had been accustomed under Hitler. In other words, I merely foresaw a state of things which the actual developments in Europe have not thus far contradicted.

I will now show how this declaration furnished me with a means of adhering with more firmness to the position I wanted France to take of non-participation in the war on the side of Germany. I was resolved never to waver on this point,

* See in this regard the attacks of de Brinon, spokesman for the collaborationist parties, found in his secret letter to Goebbels, May 11, 1943 (Berlin Archives), Appendix VI.

and my attitude brought down upon me the ferocious attacks of political groups and of members of the Paris Press, at the time of the American landing in Normandy. It was because I had already spoken with audacity that I was able, at this decisive moment, when words were to have an immediate effect, to speak the language of neutrality as it was employed in the declaration I made over the radio on D-day. Let my pronouncement on this crucial occasion be compared with what the Marshal said and it will be seen which of the two showed the greater independence toward the German occupation forces.

Is there a Prime Minister or a Minister of Foreign Affairs who, during such long and critical years, never spoke the slightest word under stress and duress of circumstances which, when separated from historical events, might later appear as excessive? None of the words I spoke have cost France anything. On the contrary, many of them permitted me to sustain and maintain her interests more effectively, at a time when they were in dire peril.

CHAPTER 13

THE AMERICAN LANDINGS IN NORTH AFRICA

HITLER'S OFFER OF AN ALLIANCE WITH FRANCE

I CANNOT refrain from crying out my indignation at the charge that 'because I hoped for a German victory I wished to help Germany in a military sense, but, not being able to obtain arms, I furnished in its stead French manpower'.

I have already shown conclusively, I hope, that I made every possible human effort to forestall the departure to Germany of French workers and to reduce these departures to a minimum. I now deal with the baseless accusation that I wished to give military aid to Germany. A charge of this sort proves total ignorance of the historical facts on the part of my accusers.

During my preliminary hearings I explained to the examining magistrate the circumstances under which I drafted a letter to Hitler, dated 22 November 1942, in which I requested a meeting with him to examine measures of collaboration in North Africa. Among other things, this letter, which was in the drafting stage and which probably was never dispatched, contained statements that proved that this collaboration was made contingent upon the assurance of moral and political conditions in France which, in advance, rendered any collaboration in North Africa impossible of realisation. I explained in detail to the Judge the reasons which determined my decision to write to Hitler and they were sufficient to justify and to explain my initiative in this sense. My object was simple: to gain time and to save France from

the immediate and frightful indignities which threatened
her at that hour. What Frenchman in full possession of all
the facts would criticise me for this course? Here are the
facts:

On 8 November, at dawn, the American troops landed in
North Africa. On this same day, at 2:50 p.m., the German
Minister in Vichy, Herr Krugg von Nidda, brought me a
message from Hitler. It was an offer of military alliance.

It was couched in these terms. The following text will be
found in the archives of the Ministry of Foreign Affairs:

On 8 November 1942, at 2:50 p.m., Herr Krugg von Nidda
communicated the following message to President Laval:

> 'Chancellor Hitler wishes to know whether the French
> Government is disposed to fight on the side of Germany
> against the Anglo-Saxon powers. In view of the latest
> Anglo-Saxon aggression a rupture by France of diplomatic
> relations with the Anglo-Saxon powers will not be re-
> garded as sufficient by the German Government. France
> will have to declare war on the English and on the Ameri-
> cans. If the French Government is prepared to adopt a
> clear-cut policy Germany is prepared to march side by side
> with France through thick and thin.'

Krugg von Nidda was instructed to obtain at once a positive reply to this question, a question of the highest historical
significance.

He enjoined me to observe the strictest secrecy. In pre-
senting the message he was most enthusiastic and optimistic
and was bitterly disappointed when I adopted an attitude of
the greatest reserve. It was quite clear that my reply would
be in the negative, but I promised to discuss Hitler's message
with the Marshal at once.

I reported almost immediately to the Marshal, expressing
spontaneously the view that we should courteously but positively turn down this offer. I added that I did not feel that it
was necessary even to consult the Council of Ministers. This
was also the Marshal's view.

Towards the end of the afternoon Krugg von Nidda returned, not for the purpose of obtaining my reply to the message, but to inform me that Chancellor Hitler would expect me to meet him at Munich the following day, that is, on 9 November 1942, at 11 p.m. I would find Abetz at the Prefecture in Dijon and he would accompany me to Munich. In actual fact, we ran into a heavy snowstorm and reached Munich only at five o'clock in the morning. Ambassador Abetz, while we waited at Dijon, asked me what reply I was carrying to Hitler and when I told him it was in the negative he was surprised and deeply disappointed. He did not disguise from me that 'this refusal of an alliance after the desertion of large bodies of French troops in North Africa might create a new and extremely dangerous situation for France'. He also confided his fears for his own person should he have to admit failure to Hitler, whose reaction would doubtless be terrible.

I could not help but wonder what my own reception would be under these circumstances. As we started on this expedition I thought to myself that I must be prepared to face any eventuality, even the worst. Indeed, I was so uncertain of the future that I took the precaution, before leaving, of destroying many of my most important documents. Perhaps the fateful sentence which I had been led to pronounce on that one occasion on 22 June 1942, to which I have already referred, might serve some purpose, but, useful as it was to defend our interests, I did not fancy it as a very effective lightning-conductor. During the long hours of our journey through the Black Forest I was haunted by a single question, which finally became an obsession. What would be the German reprisals for this refusal of an alliance?

If, in 1941, the Wehrmacht shot a dozen hostages in reprisal for the murder of a single German soldier, what price would Hitler force our country to pay in terms of bloodshed for the 'desertion' of an army whose chiefs and officer-cadres had, for the most part, been released from German prison camps? During the course of my public life I had defended France's interests in Washington, in London, in Moscow, in Rome, and in many other capitals. But never had I had a mission equal to this in difficulty and in supreme importance for my country.

Upon our arrival in Munich I was informed that I would meet Hitler at 8 a.m. I had to wait two hours before I was ushered into his office, where he was in conference with Count Ciano. Ambassador Abetz had informed him in advance of my refusal of his tender of an alliance and not once during our conversation did he allude to his offer of alliance. He stated with great vigour and apparent sincerity that he 'would chase the Anglo-Saxons from North Africa'.

'You must know that France, from this day forth, will be permitted to keep only those portions of her Empire which she is able to defend,' he told me.

He spoke in violent anger of General Giraud's escape. At this point Count Ciano intervened in the conversation, claiming bases for the Italian Air Force in the region of Constantine, to which I replied sharply. We had a violent altercation.

Hitler did not join the discussion between Ciano and myself and ended the interview shortly after. It had been brief and not particularly tempestuous on Hitler's side. It is possible that Hitler still hoped that some, at least, of the French armed forces would resist the Anglo-American landing. About 4 a.m. Abetz woke me up to tell me that the German army had crossed the demarcation line and that the Italian army was occupying a large sector of France. Ambassador Abetz begged me, so greatly was he worried by the consequences of our refusal of a German alliance and by my general attitude, to temper my protest against this double invasion.

Abetz was, I must admit, the German who understood France the best. I grant him this, with the qualification that his first interest was to serve his country completely and, at times, even brutally. He paid for his opposition to the policies applied by his Government against France by dismissal from office a few weeks later. He was accused of failing to obtain results from the policy of collaboration with France. For a long period he was not permitted to return to Paris.

It is therefore a matter of historical record that on 8 November 1942 I declined the German offer of an alliance with France and refused to declare war on the Anglo-Saxons.

It is clear, then, that the State Prosecutor was ignorant of all these facts.

I cite a further fact which bears out my case. In 1943, when the Germans organised a Waffen S.S. unit composed of 'Frenchmen' recruited from the extreme parties of collaboration, that is to say, from my most violent enemies, I obtained from the Germans the promise, borne out by a document now held under seal, that they would under no circumstances employ this unit on a front where French troops might be engaged, that is to say, in the western theatre of operations.

On 17 November 1942 Herr Schleier, the German Chargé d'Affaires, served a virtual ultimatum upon the Marshal and myself demanding that we declare war on America at once and recruit foreign legions for service in Africa. The Marshal was, moreover, told that he must denounce publicly the African 'desertions'. We were given twenty-four hours to reply. It was added that if at the expiration of this time limit we had not made a favourable reply the armistice might be broken and France be administered like Poland.

I do not recall whether the Marshal 'denounced the desertions', but I replied with a flat negative to the German demand that we declare war on America and this negative reply was approved by the Council of Ministers. I have very convincing evidence to confirm the stand which I took at that time. Herr Schleier remarked that same evening to a member of the Cabinet: 'We are not going to get anywhere with President Laval.'

My reply to that demand that we recruit legions for service in Africa was simply that our army had been dissolved and that I did not see how it could be reconstituted; moreover,

that our refusal to declare war carried with it the implication
that military collaboration, as had been suggested, was out of
the question. At long last the Germans got nothing out of
this round but the assistance of a handful of Doriot's P.P.F.
followers in Tunis.

At no time did I consider military collaboration with
Germany. I never issued any order of a military nature. I
repeatedly protested at the German Embassy against the
powers which Herr Rahn had assumed in Tunis and delegated to Guilbaud. I repeatedly stated that our authority
in Tunis was gone, and I refused, despite repeated German
demands, to cover with my approval the orders which Admiral Nateva received from them and which he could not
avoid. Following the withdrawal from office of Admiral
Darlan the Marshal assumed command of our military and
naval forces and, had I been obligated to intervene in any
manner whatsoever in a military operation, it would have
been merely to transmit his orders.

On 27 November 1942 Krugg von Nidda, accompanied by
Rochat, arrived in Chateldon at four o'clock in the morning
and, despite the fearful cold, refused to cross the threshold
of my home until 4:30 because he had received formal orders
not to see me before this hour. He notified me that the
German army had received orders to seize our fleet at Toulon
and that this operation had taken place at four o'clock this
same morning.

If it had been true that I wished to extend military aid
to Germany, surely the German Government would not have
treated me with such suspicion at a moment like this. All
these facts, which can easily be confirmed, go to prove that,
contrary to what is stated in the Act of Accusation, I never
dreamed of giving military assistance to Germany. On the
contrary, it is crystal clear that I personally and positively
rejected every offer and demand of the Germans for military
collaboration.

A simple reading of the Paris Press of this period will
reveal how bitterly I was attacked. All through my term in

office I was to be tracked by a pack of fanatical opponents. Whenever the extreme collaboration parties, notably the P.P.F., held meetings such as those at the Velodrome d'Hiver it was not General de Gaulle who was attacked. The cry which was raised was 'Laval to the stake', alternated with 'Doriot to power'.

It will be necessary only to glance through the reports, at the Prefecture of Police, of these meetings in order to determine the atmosphere prevailing. It will be quite clear that this chorus of hostility can be traced to German inspiration. How, then, can the accusation which is made against me to-day be reconciled with the consistent hostility of the collaborationist parties towards me during these years?

The Germans, at least, never had any doubts regarding my real sentiments.* They well knew that whenever I paid lip-service to them it coincided closely with their pressures and threats and formed a chapter in a methodical plan to defend French interests which they were not long in discovering and which often made it difficult for them to take the steps against us they wished to take.

On 6 June 1944 I read a message over the radio. It brought down on my head a violent Press campaign in the Occupied Zone and a furious attack by the collaboration parties.

A manifesto was drawn up bearing the signatures of several ministers, the chiefs of the collaborationist parties, several journalists, and other personalities. This manifesto was deposited at the German Embassy for dispatch to Hitler. A simple re-reading of this document ** will illustrate the degree of hostility aroused against me by my refusal to declare war and my refusal to resort to any steps against the *maquis*. Admiral Platon saw to it that the Marshal received this manifesto. I immediately summoned a meeting of the Council of Ministers which Déat, of course, failed to attend,

* See in Appendix XI two references made in *The Goebbels Diaries* concerning Pierre Laval.

** The text of this document will be found in Appendix VII.

and in my turn denounced the authors of this document.*

This manifesto, with its 400 signatures, was vigorously supported by the Germans and proves without a shadow of doubt what my attitude was. It is convincing proof of everything which I have said heretofore.

I never wished to declare war on the Allies and in order to avoid this I had to stand up against every form of pressure. I never wished to give military aid to the Germans and I never bowed to their blackmail. I refused to hand over the political direction of my country to a band of adventurers and I served as a barrier to their designs. I reduced the suffering of the French people by whittling down the successive German demands.

Surely I must have the right to reply to those who accuse me, that I consistently acted as a good Frenchman and as head of a Government faithfully anxious to preserve the higher interests of our country. Have I not the right to claim that my activity facilitated the course of those Frenchmen who, arms in hand, fought for our liberation? If only I had had a chief with greater understanding, greater loyalty, and greater political sense than the Marshal possessed, my role would have been far easier and less unhappy.

Let men of goodwill, now that they are in full possession of the facts, admit that the Resistance benefited from the fullest measure of aid that I could give it in the difficult and dramatic situation in which I was obliged to operate. Happily, I have not had to wait until now for militant resistance to thank me for services, the full nature of which they could only guess. Many a time word has been brought to me from the Resistance lines: 'If only you will continue to hold the fort!'

How can they reconcile this attitude, which was so frequently reported to me during the dark days of enemy occupation, with the sadistic desire for vengeance which is

* The secret minutes of this meeting, heretofore unpublished, will be found in Appendix VIII.

echoed in the monstrous Accusation trumped up against me by the State Prosecutor?

I experienced hours of the darkest discouragement and days of heartrending difficulty. But I remained on the bridge, determined to sink with the ship if necessary because this was the path of duty. I had no weapons that I could use against the Germans when they harried our land, nothing with which to fight them but my intelligence and strength of will. There were forty million Frenchmen to be protected and preserved.

Could I hesitate an instant to employ words and phrases which bound nobody but myself when I knew that such words and phrases would help and might even save my country?

Those about me understood my purpose perfectly well. I used to explain all this to my trusted fellow-workers without fear of any leakage to the Germans, though there were German ears and pro-German ears everywhere. My course was clear and based on political realities. It was the only course which could be followed in those tragic days. It might be a useful commentary to trace, in a line or two, the action of the Soviets during the time that they were the allies of the Germans, knowing full well that a war with their allies of to-day was inevitable to-morrow.

A striking illustration will be found in the statements, gestures, and even acts of Stalin and Molotov which served the interests of their country and their army at the time, but which had a curious sound when a new situation was created. They had to gain time to prepare for war.

I had to use similar words and to follow a similar policy in order to delay and reduce the immediate dangers and to attempt to heal the wounds which the Occupation was inflicting upon us. My words should be squarely placed within the framework of the circumstances under which I uttered them in order that they may be understood and finally approved.

Once more, I shall repeat what I said to the schoolteachers at Vichy on 3 September 1942:

'I have had to use words which have gone very far indeed, as far as words can go, but I wish you to understand, and I am certain that you do, that I am willing to run every risk and to expose myself to every attack in order to save France to-day.'

I sincerely hope that this explanatory sentence will always be bracketed with the 'hope' which I expressed on that other critical occasion on 5 June 1942. There will be then no doubt as to my intentions, though it is commonplace that good faith is not a normal thing in a period of history when passions blind the wisest men. I shall, therefore, 'drive the nail home' this last time, and truth will out. My views are clearly set forth here for men of goodwill to contemplate, in the present and in the years to come.

Call into question if you will my good sense, my political sagacity or statesmanship, but not my patriotism.

It is a sad and sorry experience to serve one's country when she is down and out, but is it not also the best proof of love and loyalty? Who dare suggest that I ever loved her less than those who stand as my accusers? Have I not, too, a better right, a more cogent reason for such devotion? All the days of my manhood have been spent in her service. In her days of prosperity and in her darkest hours I was her spokesman. To-day I am deprived of liberty, but I have gained this knowledge: Patriotism is a religion which can break prison bars, and the gloom of the cell from which I write is enlightened by this faith.

On peut tout contre moi. Je suis privé de ma liberté — mais j'ai appris que le patriotisme est la seule forme de religion qui résiste à l'emprisonnement. C'est en écrivant ces lignes que je prouve ce sentiment dans ma cellule —

CHAPTER 14

TOULON AND THE CARIBBEAN FLEET

IT IS as easy for me to reply to the Accusation that with Marshal Pétain I preferred to have the fleet destroyed at Toulon rather than to permit it to play a role which might have aided France and France's allies. My reply is simple. The fact is that I had nothing to do with the fleet at Toulon except that, on 27 November 1942 after the event, I received the message from Krugg von Nidda, the German Minister, informing me that it was surrounded by the German military forces.

Admiral Darlan alone had jurisdiction and command over the navy, including the fleet at Toulon, until he was overtaken by the Anglo-American landing at Algiers. Thereafter the Marshal had the exclusive control of our military forces on land, at sea, and in the air.

As a consequence, I had no orders to give to the fleet at Toulon. When the Admiral was at Vichy I had jurisdiction over the civilian ministries only, without any authority to concern myself with military questions. At all events, these were reduced to a minimum after 11 November 1942, when the Germans crossed the line of demarcation, because the army was dissolved. It appeared at that time, but for a short time only, that the fleet was saved.

Immediately upon being informed by Krugg von Nidda at Chateldon on 27 November, at 4:30 a.m., that our fleet had been surrounded an hour before by a German force which was to seize our ships, I registered an indignant protest. At once I set out for Vichy in great haste to confer with the Marshal and his ministers. Admiral Leluc tried to communicate by telephone with Admiral Marquis, the Maritime Prefect at Toulon, and we were informed that explosions had begun aboard the ships at four o'clock that morning and had continued without interruption thereafter. The fleet was scuttled. Admiral Laborde, chief of the naval staff, was still at his post on the *Strasbourg*. He refused to leave his post and planned to go down with his ship. He quitted his post only after the Marshal specifically ordered him to do so. The Marshal being his chief, he could accept orders from him only.

I never gave any order to Admiral Laborde, either directly or indirectly, to scuttle our warships. Admiral Darlan issued this order to all our ships following the Armistice. It was doubtless renewed from time to time. Certainly the order was never cancelled.

Every captain in the navy was under specific orders to prevent the seizure of his ship by any foreign power whatever. Prior to the Armistice the Government had entered into an agreement with the British Government never to surrender the fleet to the Germans. The surrender terms of Rethondes provided that we might keep our fleet, but on condition that we should never allow it to fall into the hands of Germany's enemies. We were thus doubly-bound and this doubtless was the motive for Admiral Darlan's order directing the scuttling of any ship which was in danger of being seized by a foreign power.

In Algiers and in London it was easy enough to speak of the Allied cause, as it is in the year 1945 in Paris now that the Germans are gone. But when the Germans were everywhere in control and the sword of Damocles was dangling over our heads, threatening a reign of terror in case the Armistice Convention was repudiated, it was not so easy for the Government in power to act as the prosecution to-day would like us to have acted.

This was impossible, not only because we had signed the Armistice and entered into agreement under it, but because France was occupied from end to end. She was without arms, without a military force, and at the mercy of a cruel victor. Action such as is recommended at this safe distance by the prosecution would have resulted in the crucifixion of our country. It may be objected that if the Marshal could not have acted otherwise than he did—and it must be repeated that he alone was responsible for the conduct of the fleet— the ships could have attempted to escape. This operation was risky—the technicians said at the time that it was impossible. Nevertheless, several units did make the attempt.

I was heartbroken when I learned of these events. Our fleet was the last remaining pride of our country. When I headed the Government in normal times I gave every support to the Minister of Marine and aided him in obtaining credits from the Chambers, sometimes, I must admit, by stretching the Parliamentary rules not a little, for the construction of ships of the *Dunkerque* class. For example, M. Charles Dumont, Minister of Marine, on one occasion, thanked me by letter, expressing his profound gratitude for my assistance. This letter I have always prized as one of my particular treasures, testifying as it does to a great service rendered to my country. The scuttling of our fleet at Toulon seemed to me to be one of the most tragic episodes of our defeat. We should have to begin all over again from scratch. Our most beautiful ships were gone. The scuttling, which spelled irreparable loss for us, was the symbol of our misfortune.

Referring now to the accusation that I would have preferred to have our Caribbean fleet sunk, our planes set afire, and our gold reserve sunk rather than surrender them to the Allies, I shall, instead of repeating myself, set forth the answer I made to the examining magistrate during one of my rare pre-trial hearings.

Here is my answer:

Your question has brought to my knowledge the names of the units of our war and merchant fleet which were stationed in the Antilles at the time of the Armistice. All these ships had been immobilised there ever since. You have informed me also that we possessed in the Antilles 107 American-manufactured planes, and finally you have reminded me that the portion of the gold reserve of the Bank of France transferred in June 1940 to Martinique represented a value of exactly twelve billion francs.

You asked me why, together with the Naval Secretary of State and Marshal Pétain, I sent telegrams to Admiral Robert, at different times, after 6 January 1943, requesting him to scuttle his ships, destroy his planes, and sink the gold of the Bank of France.

I wish first to comment upon the expression, 'sink the gold', which you have used. There was no question of sinking the gold. This would have meant its loss. On the contrary, *our intention was to have it immersed* so that, subsequently, at any time, it could be salvaged. And now I wish to state that far from having forgotten the sending of these dispatches I remember also perfectly well the reasons which led me to act as I did.

The question you put to me is directly connected with the problem of the Armistice and the obligations which it entailed upon us. I did not sign the Armistice Convention nor did I belong to the Government which asked for an armistice. From the time it was signed it became evident that the German Government would invoke its clauses on every occasion when this was to their advantage.

The second paragraph of Article 10 is worded as follows:

'The French Government will also prevent the members of French armed forces from leaving its territory and will see to it that neither arms nor equipment, ships nor planes, are transferred to England or to any other foreign country.'

When war was declared between Germany and the United States at the close of the year 1941, I was not a member of the French Government. Germany immediately became greatly concerned about our fleet, our planes, and the gold at Martinique. I became aware of the German demands only

some time after. I note that the first telegram which I sent
to Admiral Robert was dated 6 January 1943, according
to the text of his reply dated 8 January, which you quoted
in your question. I assume that the colonial and naval
secretaries had long before given instructions to Admiral
Robert and I have no doubt that they were forced to give
these instructions as a result of demands formulated by
Germany in application of the Armistice clauses. If the Germans subsequently applied to me, as well as to Marshal
Pétain, it was solely because they desired to have the orders
sent by the ministers confirmed by the Head of the State and
the Head of the Government.

As to the fleet, it was placed directly under Admiral
Darlan's orders and, subsequently, under those of Marshal
Pétain; never did I exercise any control over it. I knew, of
course, that an irrevocable order had been given, once and
for all, enjoining every ship commander to scuttle his vessel
rather than to let it fall into the hands of any foreign power.
This order applied to all foreign powers without any exception. The Germans might, and should, have contented themselves with this comprehensive and precise order. However,
they well knew that the commander of any vessel would be
unhappy in ordering the destruction of his ship and they
foresaw that the proximity of America would be a strong
temptation, and might allow our fleet in the Antilles to
evade this order.

We had among our warships a light cruiser which was
exceptionally fast, the *Emile Bertin*. The Germans would not
for the world have had it utilised against their own forces.
They came to me invoking the Armistice Convention and insisting that they would not tolerate it that the French Government should not take every disposition to prevent such a
flagrant violation of Article 10 of the Armistice. The steps
taken by the German Embassy with this object in view were
always backed up by imperative telegrams from Berlin.

In telegraphing to Admiral Robert I added nothing to the
dispatch he had already received from his minister, but I gave

a purely formal satisfaction to the Germans. A move such as this one spared us the sort of sanctions to which their methods had accustomed us. I was not personally acquainted with Admiral Robert; I knew only that his minister described him as our most intelligent Admiral, possessing, among other qualities, those of a good diplomat. I could not doubt that, upon receiving a telegram from the Marshal, myself, or the ministers, he would realise under what conditions and in what circumstances it had been written, by whom the message had been suggested, and who had insisted upon its being sent.

It is sufficient to re-read these telegrams to grasp their inner meaning, which could not escape the shrewd comprehension of Admiral Robert. As for me, I understood perfectly the meaning of the answers he sent. When he asked to defer the time for the destruction I was certain that I should learn, soon after, that he had voluntarily placed himself in a position where it would be impossible to carry out the destruction of his ships and planes and the immersion of the gold. I could not felicitate him on his attitude by telegram, for the Germans would have read the telegram, but I did not conceal my gratitude when he returned to Vichy. From the outset I have stated as a foregone conclusion, since an Armistice Convention had been signed and France had been occupied, that the Government could not escape such painful obligations. Fortunately, we found, at so great a distance, an officer sufficiently intelligent and intuitive to understand the servitude under which the French Government laboured and to realise his personal duty towards France and her navy. I might speak in the same terms of Admiral Godefroy who, in spite of Admiral Darlan's early orders, certainly issued under constraint, saved our ships which were in Alexandria. To conclude this inquiry concerning the ships, I want to point out that Admiral Robert was ordered to scuttle his vessels in the very first telegram he received. Accordingly my subsequent instructions could not, in any way, modify this order, which was a purely formal one but which allowed me to play upon the patience of the Germans up to the day when they could no longer exercise pressure upon us. The terms in which I expressed myself in the sequel are of little importance. Admiral Robert and I had mutually understood each other. Our language always reflected the same thought.

Before concluding this declaration I should like to recall that not only was I careful to preserve our ships and planes but that I had particular care for the conservation of our gold. Impoverished by war, ruined by enemy occupation, our gold reserves scattered throughout the world constituted a resource which I knew might one day facilitate the reconstruction of our country. We had an impressive amount of our gold reserve in West Africa. Is it necessary to remind you that the Germans were aware of it and often insisted that this gold should be returned to France? I always opposed a firm denial to any such proposition. I knew that they would immediately seize this gold, of which they were in so great need. I had all the more reason to protect this French asset because—and I have a right to say so—it was thanks to the policy of drastic and rigorous economy instituted by me as Head of the Government in 1935 that a large part of the world's gold flowed back into the vaults of the Bank of France. Thanks to what is left of our gold thus acquired, the French Government can proceed to-day with the purchase of goods and foodstuffs necessary to resume the material welfare of France.

Such was my reply to the examining magistrate.

As far as the planes and vessels were concerned the charge made always proceeds from the same system, which consists, on the part of the Accusation, in ignoring the existence of the Armistice Convention. It is impossible to conceive how a Government in France could have avoided giving these orders. It is natural that the Germans took advantage of Article 10 of the Convention to insist upon these orders.

As they possessed our cypher it was impossible to communicate with Admiral Robert without their knowledge. But the question of prime importance does not lie in the transmission of these orders but in their execution, and they were *not* executed. Our ships were not sunk and our planes were not destroyed. But the Accusation still retains against me an alleged intention.

Admiral Robert returned to France. He understood perfectly that he did not have to obey the orders we had been obliged to give. *He was not blamed; he was, on the contrary, congratulated by me.* Every honour was bestowed upon him.

What, then, remains of the criminal intentions attributed to me?

I was successful, at the same time, in respecting the Armistice terms and in saving the Antilles fleet. We succeeded in escaping the harsh reprisals which the Germans would inevitably have imposed on France, without losing a single vessel or a single plane. Is it possible to conceive of a policy more in conformity with our best interests?

I have already dismissed the accusation that I conspired with Marshal Pétain to enter into an open alliance with the Axis. Never in my life had I supposed that we could or would or should have a military alliance with Germany. It never entered into my wildest dreams that we could contemplate an alliance with our enemy. I have shown that the principal objective of my foreign policy was to keep France out of war. This is why, after having resisted every form of German pressure following upon Mers el Kebir, Dakar, and Madagascar, I rejected the German offer of an alliance, made on 8 November 1942, an alliance through 'thick and thin'.

I never took the slightest heed of the German demands that we declare war on England and on the United States.

Had anyone taken the trouble to ask me I might have contributed some interesting side-lights on the history of our country during the Occupation. I might have recalled that, while he was in power and I was not, Admiral Darlan travelled to Berchtesgaden to confer with Hitler. The purpose of this conference was to consider a vast project for military collaboration, in fact a real alliance with Germany. Curiously, it was at this time that certain French generals, who were prisoners of war, were liberated in order to carry out certain special military missions.

The plan was to formulate, in common with the Germans, certain schemes for the recapture of our colonies. Bizerta and the Tunisian railway-lines were to be opened to German traffic in order that Rommel's army might be regularly supplied.

Admiral Darlan requested, in exchange for this military collaboration and the reversal of our alliance, the liberation of our prisoners, the reduction of the Occupation costs and the suppression of the demarcation line.

Probably we should have had about the same terms had I accepted Hitler's offer of an alliance, contained in his message to me of 8 November 1942.

Darlan's pourparlers, which remained secret, led to no result. Rommel's army, which had been threatened, had meanwhile recovered, and, as a consequence, Germany's need for an arrangement no longer existed.

Had I been in office at that time I should not have agreed to any scheme of this sort. I should have been willing to make peace with Germany only in order to obtain concrete advantages for France. I should never have consented to pay for peace in terms of French blood spilled in the same cause as German blood; that is to say, at the price of a military alliance with Germany. Without any doubt Germany never abandoned this hope of an alliance with France and there was a project—I learned of this during my deportation to Germany—for another visit to Hitler in 1941 on the part of Admiral Darlan. At this juncture, however, the Anglophile element got the upper hand in the Wilhelmstrasse. Hitler was then dreaming his dream of *Mein Kampf*—an alliance with England at the expense of France.

CHAPTER 15

ALSACE-LORRAINE

THE Accusation charges me with giving an interview to Mr. Heinzen, correspondent of the United Press, on 25 May 1941, in Paris. Only one paragraph of this interview, which refers to Alsace-Lorraine, is quoted.

Although I was not in office at the time, I agreed to give this interview in order to answer a radio-broadcast delivered by Admiral Darlan two days before, actually on 23 May at 1 p.m. Ever since 13 December 1940 I had remained silent, neither writing nor speaking, and I was most painfully shocked when I heard Darlan say that upon the result of the negotiations he was then carrying on depended 'the life or the *death*' of France. These are his own words: 'It is necessary for her to choose between life or death.' Another statement shocked me even more, it was: 'In June 1940 the victor might have refused the Armistice, crushed us and *wiped France off the map of the world. This he did not do.*' I answered Admiral Darlan by stating to the United Press that: '*I knew France to be eternal and that she would regain her place, her entire place, on the map of the world.*' This statement was part of the interview. Is there not a striking contrast between those two declarations, Darlan's and mine? Do they not express two different ways of thinking, two different policies, and two ways of speaking in the presence of Hitler?

We must not forget that the statement was made in Paris in 1941 and not in 1945. Germany had then completed a *de facto* annexation of Alsace-Lorraine. Darlan had returned from Berchtesgaden and had declared in the same speech: 'The Chancellor did not ask me for any colonial territory.' The Admiral was careful to refrain from making any allusion to our own territorial soil, and I had every reason to fear (to-day I know that my fear was justified) that Darlan,

149

in exchange for military co-operation which was to entail the liberation of all our war prisoners and the suppression of the demarcation line, had accepted as an accomplished fact the annexation of Alsace by Germany. This was of the utmost gravity and I searched my mind for a formula which would bring the problem of our two provinces into the open.

I was, of course, obliged to use much prudence in my choice of words lest the German censorship interfere with their publication. It was then that I invented the metaphor of children not yet of age who, upon reaching majority, could choose the life they were to lead. It is clear, therefore, that *I did not accept the annexation,* for my statement on Alsace-Lorraine ends with these words: 'It is a delicate and grave problem which can only be presented and solved in an atmosphere of friendly understanding between two great neighbouring countries.' If one re-reads the text of the interview to-day it is clear that, according to the opinion I then expressed, Alsace and Lorraine 'upon reaching majority' were to choose their own fate. It is a fact well known to us that they wanted to remain French. They had often expressed themselves in this connection. I well know that no lasting peace is possible with Germany if a scrap of our territory is taken away from us. I never conceived of any collaboration with our neighbours unless both Alsace and Lorraine were to remain French. I expressed this opinion in the course of my interview when I stated that: 'I presented myself to the Germans as a peasant obstinately rooted in his own soil, determined to defend his land.'

When I recalled the fact that Alsace and Lorraine had always been at the core of our conflicts with Germany I was merely stating an historical truth. When I added that I feared the possible application of this historical law I merely envisaged the hypothesis of peace terms imposed by Germany and not that of a peace based upon goodwill and the mutual desire for reaching an understanding.

All this meant that France could never willingly give up Alsace and Lorraine. It meant that she would lose those two

provinces only in the event of peace terms imposed upon her
by force. In short, it meant exactly the reverse of what I
am charged with by the Accusation.

The Germans themselves did not make any mistake about
what I meant. The Wehrmacht censorship, which functioned
in Paris at the time, immediately forbade the publication of
the paragraph of my interview concerning Alsace. I protested
vigorously at the German Embassy, refusing to release the
whole interview, and towards the end of the evening I
learned that after many difficulties the prohibition had been
lifted. Mr. Heinzen can confirm all this.

It was the first time since the Armistice that a French statesman in the Occupied Zone had dared to raise publicly the
issue of Alsace-Lorraine and to claim our right to all our territory. The prosecution would indeed have liked me to use
plainer and more brutal language, but who can pretend that
it would have been possible for me, at that time, to go
further and more daringly along such a path?

The people of Alsace made no mistake about the meaning
of my words. They interpreted them as a gleam of hope at
the very time when military events seemed to have plunged
them into the deepest distress. I received from many of them
expressions of gratitude and thanks for a stand which, according to them, implied real courage. Russia was still Germany's ally. America had not yet entered the war, and I must
repeat that, upon his return from Berchtesgaden, Darlan had
made the statement to which I have already alluded.

The worst interpretation that could possibly be given to
my words might be that they suggested a possible autonomy
for the two provinces, but such an inference would be a
false one because, in fact, neither Alsace nor Lorraine would
ever consent to separate from France if they were given the
right to choose their own regime.

As to the question of autonomy, my position on this subject has always been well known. Back in 1926, as Minister
of Justice, I directed under Aristide Briand the department
of Alsace-Lorraine at the time when the famous autonomist

manifesto was published. Notwithstanding the advice of my
chief, who advocated moderation because he feared an aggra-
vation of the incident and the spreading of a conflict between
the autonomists and the other Alsatians, I did not hesitate to
punish very severely all officials—and they were very numerous—who had signed the manifesto. My only difficulty was
with a city notary of Ville, as I did not have the legal authority to deprive him of office. I therefore ordered the
Attorney-General, M. Fachot, to dismiss him under the
threat of himself being discharged within three days.

The Germans knew my sentiments towards Alsace-Lorraine, not only because I never ceased to protest against the
measures of force taken against these provinces, which violated the Armistice Convention, but also because I never
neglected to avail myself of every opportunity to state that
no real peace would ever be possible between our two countries on such a basis.

Through the Armistice Convention the Government filed
more than seventy protests against the German violations of
the clauses of the Armistice with reference to Alsace-Lorraine,
and after April 1942, when I returned to power, I made
solemn protest to the German Government against the *de
facto* annexation. This protest was handed by me to the
German Ambassador and it served as a basis for all the
claims and protests which were later made.

I am aware that we have been criticised for not having
given more publicity to our protestation. I do not know
what would have happened if we had done so. One thing
remains certain: such a move would inevitably have led the
Germans to increase their harshness and brutality against
our compatriots of Alsace-Lorraine.

Among my documents which were seized and placed under
seal there is a letter, dated October 1944, which I addressed
to the editor of the *Geneva Tribune,* in which my opinion upon this subject is explained, but the conditions of
constraint to which I was subjected when in Germany prevented me from mailing the letter. In this document I pro-

tested with indignation against the allegation of a Belgian newspaper-man who wrote that I would have been ready to exchange Alsace-Lorraine for the Belgian province of Wallonie.

I might recall that during the conversation I had with Marshal Goering in March 1942, which I have already referred to, and during which he showed himself so bitter against France, I did not fear to tell him that the problem of Alsace-Lorraine was not essential for Germany, whereas it was vital to France and constituted the cornerstone of any agreement between our two countries.

I remember the visit of M. Frey, Mayor of Strasbourg, to Vichy, who will testify to this. He and his colleagues were then in Perigueux. He described the hardships suffered by his compatriots and spoke these words which touched me deeply: 'I keep on telling them that I know Laval very well. He is defending us and he will continue to protect us.'

I also remember that the Great Rabbi of Strasbourg came to Vichy in order to see the Marshal. He was received by Guérard, Director of my Cabinet. As he had been informed that I was discouraged by the many difficulties which I had to deal with, some of which seemed insoluble, the Rabbi asked M. Guérard to beg me not to resign, and especially not to give up hope. The report which M. Guérard made for me on this occasion is also among my documents which were seized and placed under seal.

I have no reason to believe that either M. Frey or the Great Rabbi were merely using casual phrases of polite usage.

During the whole period of the enemy occupation I was constantly concerned with the fate of our unhappy compatriots who had taken refuge in the south-west and the centre of France. I maintained in office all the Prefects of Alsace-Lorraine in order to affirm our rights upon the three departments of their two provinces. I watchfully supervised all measures which we took to welcome the refugees from Alsace-Lorraine. I caused all the laws and decrees providing for the protection of these refugees to be enacted.

I am revolted by the unfairness of such an accusation. How could I have dreamed for one second that France would abandon Alsace-Lorraine to the victor?

It is now realised that I returned to power in 1942 under the most tragic circumstances and in order to protect our country and to lighten its sufferings.

M. Pinot, former Commissioner for our war prisoners, came to see me in Vichy in a very friendly spirit and begged me to abandon power the day after the American landing in North Africa. I asked him: 'What will happen to the refugees from Alsace-Lorraine if I do?' It was in part to assure their protection that I remained in office.

I was able to prevent the deportation to Germany, as workers, of all refugees from Alsace-Lorraine. After the occupation of the Southern Zone I succeeded in persuading the Germans not to consider them as citizens of the Reich.

Had I not remained in power, and had I decided to show no more interest in Alsace-Lorraine or in the affairs of France in general, I should now be exempt from any criticism. This proves that I was right to assume all risks, including the unexpected one of being accused and having to appear before the High Court of Justice.

If the Government had not been there what would have become of the Alsatians and Lorraines in the Southern Zone when they came into contact with the Gestapo? It is evident that all of them could not have fled to the *maquis*. To the long martyrology of our two provinces numberless innocent victims would have been added. After having prevented all this, is it fair and just that I should be charged with a crime?

The day will doubtless come when my intentions will no longer be misunderstood and when my deeds will be recognised as those of a true Frenchman who, in a tragic period of enslavement, did not fear to expose himself in order to serve his country. I earned less glory than others, but the subsequent events proved that the risks assumed were not less great.

CHAPTER 16

PARIS, AUGUST 1944: MY ARREST

AFTER the landing in Normandy the defeat of the Germans in France appeared certain. Their armies unceasingly gave ground and it became evident that they would soon be obliged to abandon Paris.

I repeatedly protested to the German Embassy against deportations of French people, especially of political men. I often demanded their return, insisting especially in favour of President Herriot. I had pointed out the necessity of calling Parliament together in order that both houses might convene in a National Assembly.

Exceptional circumstances had been invoked as a reason for the reunion of 1940, which permitted the *attribution of special regular powers* to Marshal Pétain. New circumstances should have brought such powers to a conclusion, and it seemed to me indispensable that the National Assembly should take over again, through legal procedure, the powers which it had delegated to the Marshal in 1940.

On arriving in Paris, Wednesday, 9 August 1944, at 8 a.m., I was faced by three problems:

1. That of the capital's food supply;
2. That of persuading the German Government not to defend Paris;
3. That of convoking a National Assembly.

To such an Assembly I should have been able to give an account of the conditions under which the Government had been obliged to act during the Occupation. Even more important, the legal and constitutional powers of France would have been regularly transferred.

This, in my opinion, was the only way to create an atmosphere of peace and union throughout the country after the tribulations of war.

155

At an early hour in the morning I summoned to my Matignon office the heads of the Municipal Council and the members of the Departmental Council of the Seine. I confided my intentions to both these bodies, most of whom included men elected by popular vote, former Senators or Deputies.

Next day, 10 August, the following report was given out:

'Upon his arrival from Vichy, President Laval received M. Taittinger, President of the Paris City Council, and M. Constant, President of the Seine Departmental Council, together with the Boards of both assemblies. He gave the reasons which determined his return to Paris and stressed his intention to remain among the people of the Metropolis.'

Friday, 11 August, at 6 p.m., after a long conversation with a number of Parliamentarians, who joined in my way of thinking, I received at Matignon the eighty-seven Mayors of Paris and the suburban towns, the majority of the latter regularly elected by popular vote. They unanimously expressed their confidence and passed the following resolution:

'The Mayors of the Seine Department met together to assure President Laval, Head of the French Government, of their devoted friendship and deep affection. They affirm their complete confidence in his action, convinced as they are that through his love of our land he will find the way of salvation which will bring about the resurrection of France. Profoundly devoted to him personally, they are happy to give, by their cohesion, an example of union and discipline, with no other ambition than that of serving their country.'

Shortly after receiving the Mayors I had a long interview with Ambassador Abetz, to whom I expounded all the arguments in favour of President Herriot's return. The Ambassador, impressed by my arguments, informed me that I might,

if I so desired, go myself and announce to the President of
the Chamber of Deputies that he was at liberty.

On 12 or 13 August 1944, I went to Nancy to bring President Herriot back to Paris. I informed him of the negotiations I had entered into and the result obtained, and of my
desire to convoke the National Assembly according to the
legal procedure which had been laid down in the law of 1875.

After a long period of detention, Herriot was naturally,
and, I believe, agreeably surprised by the news I brought;
for he might well have feared, considering the German
methods practised and the military conditions prevailing at
that moment, that he risked deportation to Germany. Instead of leading in the direction of Berlin, here was the road
to Paris open before him.

I had obtained from the German Ambassador a guarantee
that I might remain in Paris. I had categorically refused to
move eastward. As Head of the Government, whatever risks
I ran, I considered that I had no right to abandon my
post before having effected the regular transfer of my powers.
The German Ambassador, seeing that I was resolved not to
give in, finally assented.

President Herriot installed himself at the Prefecture of the
Seine, while waiting to take over the premises belonging to
the Presidency at the Chamber of Deputies. Orders had been
given that the German services should evacuate the building
before the evening of Thursday, 17 August.

I had also to ascertain the whereabouts of M. Jeanneney,
President of the Senate. He was in the Grenoble region. On
M. Herriot's advice I saw M. Blondeau, State Counsellor and
Director of the President of the Senate's Cabinet, and asked
him if he would be willing to leave at once for Grenoble
and bring back M. Jeanneney. Telephonic communication
was then impossible, as all the circuits had been cut. This
projected journey, to which M. Blondeau consented, never
took place. (I shall call as witnesses M. Herriot and M.
Blondeau.)

At the same time I negotiated with the Germans and the

Swedish Consul that Paris should be spared all useless destruction. The same day, towards 10 p.m., the German Ambassador came to announce that the Wehrmacht would give orders that the troops were not to defend Paris. By two vigorous interventions the evening before, I had prevented the destruction of the Central Electric Station and of the telephonic power plants of the capital.

Some moments later, at about 10:30, I was informed by a telephone call from one of our own police inspectors, whom I had placed at M. Herriot's disposal, that the German police had just arrived at the Prefecture of the Seine, claiming that they had been ordered to take M. Herriot back to Maréville, near Nancy, where I had gone to fetch him some days before.

I hastened at once to the Préfecture de la Seine to protest against this new arrest, and explained to Captain Nosseck that the mission he was undertaking constituted the gravest offence against me and that I formally opposed the execution of any such project. I then called up Ambassador Abetz, asking him to come immediately to the Prefecture and confer with M. Herriot and myself. Both of us registered an energetic protest against such procedure, an absolute negation of a solemn promise. The Ambassador attempted to explain that he had taken upon himself the responsibility of setting M. Herriot at liberty, in agreement with the police authorities, but that now he had received orders from his Government to reverse this decision.

He apologised, pretending, however, that it was impossible for him to get out of obeying this order. In the hope of gaining time and of making the German Government perhaps rescind its order, I handed the Ambassador an official letter addressed to Hitler. At the same time I gave the following written protest to Abetz:

Paris, 17 August 1944.

MR. AMBASSADOR,

Having been advised by you that I might announce to M. Herriot that he was free, I hastened to Nancy to inform him of his liberation and brought him back with me to Paris.

The news that he has been again arrested and is to be taken to Nancy or into Germany affects me profoundly.

Should such an order be sustained it would constitute towards me the gravest offence—a duplicity which, as you know, is not in my nature, might be imputed to me.

I therefore request that I should be considered as your prisoner on the same grounds as President Herriot. In any case such action would place me in a position where I should be obliged to renounce immediately the exercise of my present functions.

Accept, Mr. Ambassador, the assurance, &c. . . .

PIERRE LAVAL.

Herriot, also, wrote the following letter:

To His Excellency the German Ambassador in Paris.

Paris, 16 August, 1944.

After having been informed at Nancy by President Laval that I was liberated, and this without any initiative on my part, after having been conducted back to Paris where, for prudential reasons and the general interest, I deprived myself of the liberty of which I had been assured, without committing the least act which could entail reproach or criticism, I am once more carried off towards an unknown destination, with my wife, who willingly and courageously shares my fate.

I have no means to resist force when it is exercised in opposition to a solemn pledge. But I leave this solemn protest in the hands of President Laval, Head of the Government, with the request that he transmit it to the German Ambassador in Paris.

Signed: EDOUARD HERRIOT.

It was then agreed that M. and Mme. Herriot should pass the night at the Prefecture, and next morning (17th) should go to the German Embassy where, the Ambassador told me, they would be guaranteed against any new police intervention until the arrival from Berlin of an answer to the letter I had written. It was arranged that I myself should join them at the Embassy next day at noon, which I did.

It was on this same morning of the 17th that the Prefect of Police, M. Bussière, telephoned to advise me of the departure for Germany of Déat, Darnand, and de Brinon.

Ambassador Abetz then informed me that he had just received instructions which would no longer permit him to allow M. Herriot to remain in Paris, but that he must, that very day, be again conducted to Maréville.

Once more I protested vigorously, only to learn that Abetz had also received instructions enjoining him to oblige me, together with the members of my Government, to leave for Belfort that very day. He added that the Marshal also would be forced to leave Vichy, and that the German Minister, Herr Renthe Fink, was to inform him of this decision, and to see that the order was carried out. At this point I reminded the Ambassador of the solemn pledge he had made concerning me when I had publicly announced my intention not to leave Paris, where imperious duty obliged me to remain, and where I was ready to accept all personal risks. I added that the German Government had absolutely no right thus to dispose of either my Minister or myself.

I informed him of my intention to call a Cabinet Council that afternoon, after which I would communicate to him our Government's answer. All the Ministers present at this reunion approved the protest I had filed, as well as the refusal to leave Paris, which I had opposed to the German order. I wrote immediately to the Ambassador an official letter to this effect, to which he responded that he would use force, if necessary, to execute the order he had received. I once more assembled my Ministers to inform them of this correspondence. They approved the terms of my letter to the German

Ambassador, in which I informed him that under these circumstances the Government must automatically cease to exercise its functions. Certain Ministers, MM. Cathala, Grasset, and Chassaigne confided to me their intention of remaining behind, and succeeded in hiding themselves.

At about ten o'clock the German Ambassador appeared at the Hotel Matignon, together with the Chief of the German Police. The cars of the Gestapo were lined up before the door. A notice of the order of arrest was served on me. Such were the conditions under which I was forced to leave Paris. The Prefect of Police, the Prefect of the Seine, and the Presidents of both Paris Assemblies were present. Before entering my motor, I handed to each person concerned the following instructions which I had prepared for them:

Paris, 17 August 1944.

The Head of the Government to M. Taittinger, President of the Municipality of Paris, and to M. Victor Constant, President of the Seine Departmental Council.

Forced by the German Government to leave Paris, I desire before resigning my functions to accomplish a final act.

Some days ago I expressed to you the consolation I found, during these grave hours, in being in Paris.

I considered it my duty to share the perils and to associate myself with the fate of our city.

As Head of the Government my duty naturally is to all French citizens, but more especially to those of the Capital.

I cannot forget that I have been Deputy and Senator of the Seine and that I am still Mayor of Aubervilliers, President of the Union of the Mayors of the Seine Department. I owe, consequently, a particular debt of gratitude to all those who, after having joined hands with me, have never withdrawn theirs from mine.

Tell those who for so long a time have placed in me their confidence that in the perspective which time alone can give to my actions they will understand more fully my position and the love I bear to France.

At this tragic moment I ask you to give your wholehearted support to both Prefects, René Bouffet and Amédée Bussière, in whose hands I am placing the fate of Paris.

Your legitimate influence over the Parisian population will, I am sure, enable you to assure the continuity of municipal life.

The day will come when France at peace will no longer tolerate unjust hatreds and summary judgments.

Meanwhile, in your assemblies and together with all men of goodwill, work for the unity of the French people.

Signed: PIERRE LAVAL.

Preceded and followed by the cars of the Gestapo, we were taken to Nancy where I was once more to find President Herriot. From there we were sent on to Belfort, where the Marshal was to rejoin us two days later.

I am entirely ignorant of all that may have been said or written concerning my initiative in procuring the liberation of M. Herriot, or of my desire to call a meeting of the National Assembly; I have only read, in the *Geneva Tribune,* October or November 1944, an article reproduced from a Lyons newspaper, where the facts were presented in a biased and fantastic manner.

They were exactly as I have set them down. They attest my desire and intention to abide by the constitutional laws of our country. I had naturally intended to inform the General Staff of the Allied armies then marching on Paris of my project and to let them know that MM. Jeanneney and Herriot were in Paris.

Time was not left me for this, since the Germans forced me and the Government to leave Paris. I told President Herriot that I planned also to advise Marshal Pétain in Vichy of our intention, a thing that appeared to him of lesser importance.

CHAPTER 17

DID I HUMILIATE FRANCE?

DEALING with the accusations of the State Prosecutor it would have been sufficient to establish the balance sheet of my activities and to decide whether they had been detrimental or profitable to France.

This is precisely what the prosecution did not wish to do. And I was obliged, from my cell, without sleep, with the sole aid of my memory, to make the effort necessary to oppose to their ignorance and prejudice the reality of facts.

I was even refused the authorisation to see the ministers who are at Fresnes and who could have given me necessary data and information. Deprived of the normal right of self-defence, I nevertheless succeeded in revealing the truth on essential problems and, in any case, on all the chief points contained in the Accusation. But I aim to go a step further—I wish to show what the life of France was in all its phases under enemy occupation. These are pages of history that I must present in order to defend the thousands of loyal officials who, in following my orders, were able to reduce the sufferings of the French people and sometimes even to build and restore, at the very moment when war and the enemy were destroying all about us.

Is it because the case that I was making was too clear that my presentation was suddenly interrupted? And is this the reason why my trial is being suddenly hurried to a close?

It remains for me to say what I think of the humiliation I am supposed to have brought upon France and to answer the reproach of having, by my policy, caused moral and material prejudice for which France to-day pays the price. The real crime was not that of having been present when the humiliation of defeat was inflicted upon us. The real crime was to have launched France upon a war obviously lost in advance, since no preparation, either diplomatic or military, had been made to forestall defeat.

My crime, if it were one, would have been the acceptance,

163

during the Occupation, of those burdens which in justice should have been borne by those who were responsible for our disaster. My error was to have accepted the receivership in a bankruptcy which I myself had sought by every means to avoid.

The real crime was not to have foreseen soon enough the redoubtable danger which Hitler personified and, even more terrible, to have foreseen the danger and to have done nothing to prevent it.

I did not commit these crimes, I denounced them indignantly during the years, and especially during the last months which preceded the war. I shall read at my trial the official and secret records of the sittings of the Foreign Affairs Commission of the Senate and the report of the secret committee meeting of March 1940 and then the stand I took will be clear to all the world.*

I wished, in 1931, our country to live on neighbourly terms with Germany. I then advocated understanding and agreement with Germany and even in 1935 a policy of good neighbour relations. But at the same time, knowing as I did the boundless ambition of Hitler, the growing power of his armies, his design to build the greater Reich and assure German hegemony over Europe, I also undertook by every means to encircle Germany politically.

It was with this object in view that I signed with Mussolini the Treaties of Rome. With this same end in view I facilitated the reconciliation between Italy and Yugoslavia, and persuaded Austria, in order to defend herself, to arrange for military help from Czechoslovakia, Yugoslavia, and Roumania. Again it was with this end in view that I negotiated and signed the Franco-Soviet Treaty.

The real crime was to have broken the Italian agreements. There can be no explanation nor excuse for this blunder. The consequences were immediate and disastrous: the remilitarisation of the Rhineland was the first sign of Hitler's

* See in Appendix VIII the heretofore unpublished text of the minutes of this secret meeting.

devastating enterprise. This was the immediate consequence of the breaking of the political and military agreements that I had signed with Italy.

From the very instant that Mussolini, in exasperation, threw himself into the arms of Hitler, the drama was certain to develop rapidly. Austria was annexed; Italy was the first to pay dearly for this mistake. From then on she was to have a common frontier with Germany.

The real crime was to go to Munich and explain to Hitler that he had nothing to fear from the Western powers, that he might quietly digest Austria; and in addition be offered the Sudetenland. But the ogre's appetite was insatiable. Austria was not sufficient. He annexed Czechoslovakia.

After Munich, nothing was done to renew diplomatic relations with Rome. Still worse, I was prevented from renewing my contact with Mussolini. When he realised the danger to his country of this policy he expressed through informal channels the desire to meet me. I shall read at my trial the report of a secret session of the Senate. In my interpellation of March 1939 I referred to the conversation I had had on this subject with M. Daladier, Prime Minister at that time.

And the French Government failed to turn towards Russia. All the advantages and the means of defence that could have been derived from the Franco-Soviet pact were neglected. Our Government ignored and snubbed the Soviets. The possibility was not even envisaged that their armies could move into Poland to meet the Germans in the event of a German attack against Poland.

The real crime was to follow a policy towards Russia which inevitably led the Soviets to seek a direct agreement with Germany. Ideological differences were not enough then to prevent Stalin and Hitler from reaching an agreement. That is where our Government made another mistake. It failed to realise that imperious and immediate realities must take precedence over ideological conflicts. Hitler had learned from Bismarck, and the defeat of 1918 confirmed the lesson, that the German army cannot with any prospect of victory fight a war simultaneously on the eastern and western fronts.

He wished first to attack Poland in order to recover the territory that the Versailles treaty had taken from Germany. He knew how to divide his adversaries. He was not worried about the west. All he needed was to come to terms in the east. He wished to avoid a fight with the Soviet army at all costs.

Stalin wanted peace at that time. He knew Hitler's plans to conquer the Ukraine and the Caucasus. He knew the military might of Germany. He could no longer rely upon collective security. Munich, to which he was not invited, had destroyed Geneva, and he feared that the Western Powers had abandoned the east of Europe to Hitler.

Thus, both dictators did not hesitate to sign, on August 1939, the Moscow Agreement. The Munich Pact accounts for the pact of Moscow.

The sequel is known, all too well known. Poland was attacked and rapidly smashed, and war was declared by France alone, or practically alone, as Great Britain was not at all ready. It was because the French ministers were unable to conceive the necessity for security and the essential need for a realistic foreign policy that we were drawn into a fearful adventure which we and Europe as a whole might have escaped.

I stated in March 1940, at the secret session of the Senate, amid unanimous applause, that the Government had plunged us into war—with extraordinary levity.

How, under these circumstances, can the humiliation of France be attributed to me? When I gave up the office of Prime Minister in January 1936 France and Great Britain were rivals at Geneva for first place in Europe. Our country was prosperous and happy, her budget had been successfully balanced, her currency was sound. We enjoyed every liberty. We possessed a powerful army, a fleet, an Empire, and the reserves of the Bank of France were overflowing with gold, the left bank of the Rhine was demilitarised.

Who, then, brought down calamity upon us? Hitler without doubt, but we might have neutralised and foiled his efforts. Why did irresponsible politicians succour and assist his schemes?

I was not of their number. I repeatedly denounced them. I gave voice to my indignation. I had foreseen and repeatedly declared that the policy they were following would lead us to ruin and humiliation. Our country will now be obliged to struggle through long hard years to reconquer the place she then held in the world. But how can I be reproached with the humiliation to which she was subjected through the fault of others?

On 3 September 1939, when the Government asked us to vote a special appropriation for war purposes, I moved for a secret session so as to enlighten my colleagues. France was being plunged into a war and it was both whispered and thought that she might never really have to fight out that war. I have never witnessed such incompetence and recklessness as was displayed at the start of what was soon to be called the 'phoney war'.

I am accused, despite the fact that I undertook, out of pure patriotism, to defend France against the victor of 1940, of having espoused this policy because in 1940 I believed in a German victory. It is a fact that in 1940 and for a long time thereafter a German victory was readily conceivable. If Germany had backed up her armies with an intelligent and clever foreign policy she might clearly have won the war and, in fact, had not America subsequently entered the struggle the war was won for Germany already. Russia was still Germany's ally. But we! What could we do? Our country was overrun, we were crushed by the victor.

When France's fate is at stake the sacrifice I am prepared to make for her is limitless.

What I wished above everything was a peace which would leave intact our territory and our colonial Empire. I wanted to reduce to a minimum the sacrifices which the enemy occupation imposed upon our country.

Was that a crime? As to the language I used when talking to Hitler at Montoire, it was not that of a beaten man; I did not humble myself. I had acquired the habit, in many international conferences, of speaking a proud language appropriate for expressing the viewpoint of a country which was powerful and respected. Standing before Hitler at Montoire I denied defeat when I recalled to him the courage of our soldiers and our past victories, and said that the trial of arms in the future might once more be favourable to us.

I discussed our rights as a Frenchman should do when he speaks in the name of France.

No, I did not humiliate my country. I could not have done so. I should not have known how to do it. I defended her interests passionately. It was my only reason for being at the head of the Government. I deplored our misfortunes but I never doubted our country's future. Germany had overrun the frontiers of Europe but Russia remained intact and England was not vanquished.

Were a coherent foreign policy to be developed these countries could be used to counterbalance German hegemony. I knew that one day the weapons would fall from her hands and that, without us, she would be incapable of organising Europe.

I did not accept the injustices of which she was guilty in Europe. But we had to gain time and space, we had to recommence the patient work of organising the nations which Germany had subjugated and which were entitled to be born again. No, I never had, and never could have, the soul of a beaten man. I was not beaten myself. It was inconceivable to me that France could be defeated.

I did not then realise how far the barbarism and savagery of a regime which denied and trampled under foot all human rights could go. This in itself should be proof that I would never have accepted a system which did not safeguard all our traditions and all our interests.

In order to understand my policy during the Occupation it is essential to distinguish the two periods. When I returned to the Government in 1942 I no longer had the ideas which I advocated in 1940. The war had evolved. Russia and America were fighting Germany.

In 1940 the German Government, at least until Gauleiter Burckel expelled the inhabitants of Lorraine, had proceeded with the correctness that might be expected from a victor who respects his adversary. In 1942—and there could be no mistake as to the German attitude after my conversation with Goering—Germany intended to treat us with harshness and without any consideration or regard for the future relations between our two countries.

Why did I, then, return to power? As I have already explained, it was to defend and protect our country.

Yes, if I then committed a crime, it was a crime against myself and my dearest ones. How can I be blamed for a sacrifice made for my country's sake? How can ingratitude go further?

After all that I have said and all that still remains to be said and which a complete pre-trial hearing of my case would have brought to light, it is evident that my presence at the head of the Government permitted the saving of tens of thousands of French lives.

There is no field in which I cannot prove conclusively that the Occupation would have been infinitely more deadly and cruel had I not been there.

That is the negative aspect of my action—the aspect which does not appear—the aspect which I could not reveal when the Germans were on the spot without the risk of compromising the results.

But there is also the positive aspect, that which allowed me to keep France alive. I imagine that, since the Liberation, reports have been made on the food supplies, finances, industrial and agricultural production, transportation, postal services, in short all the branches of the State administration. If, to-day, honesty reigned, statistics and balance sheets would be published covering these years and we would not have to hear the 'Greek Chorus', constantly repeated: 'Vichy betrayed

France.' The facts and figures which I shall make public during my trial will speak for themselves. But perhaps the Government fears certain comparisons.*

I have nothing to fear from enlightened public opinion. I have worked too much, struggled too hard, suffered too much, not to want the truth to be made known.

Courageous men, honest public servants of all ranks, did not hesitate to serve during the unhappy period of the Occupation. Ministers, secretaries, great Prefects (I should like to name them all) had, like myself, no other thought than their country's welfare. They have been smitten or threatened. Why this ostracism? It can come only from ignorance of the facts and circumstances or from a desire to nourish in our country a spirit of hatred and division.

Why should those who served France be ranked with the handful of men who voluntarily placed themselves in German service? Does not France to-day need all her children, all those who are honest and courageous, to assist in her material and moral resurrection? When I examine my conscience I find no echo of reproach. No reasoning, no threat, no judgment can trouble the peace of my soul. It is pure, and unsullied by the enemy.

I am reproached with humiliating France; why not rather recognise all that I have endured for her sake?

Was it not logical that France should have a Government

* AN EXPLANATORY NOTE ADDED BY LAVAL

In 1941 a Government bureau was created to look after the welfare of war prisoners. It functioned under my own control from 1942 on. In each department a home for prisoners was established. An aid centre was opened in every town and important village. Each repatriated prisoner received a suit and a pair of shoes, each family was given an allocation. Eighteen million garments and hundreds of thousands of tons of food were sent to prisoners' camps. The annual budget of this department amounted to eighty millions. Our staff for all France comprehended 300 officials. I learn to-day that the Ministry of Prisoners has now a budget of four billions instead of eighty millions, has requisitioned dozens of buildings and engages thousands of new bureaucrats. I fear that it is the same in many other departments.

to limit the exigencies of the victor? I had no link with the Committee of de Gaulle, but it can well be imagined that we might have been in accord. He in London or Algiers, ready to participate in the Liberation and anxious to hasten V-day, and I in Vichy or Paris to protect the country, maintain our administration and the financial and economic structure of our nation.

May I cite one last hypothesis, even if it may seem somewhat absurd? Suppose the Germans had been the first to invent the atomic bomb. If they had won the war instead of losing it, with what then could I have been reproached? Should I not then have been congratulated for having held out so long in the interest of France? Nobody then would have worried over the heavy burden I had borne and the moral sufferings I had undergone. According to Léon Blum's formula, I should have been known as a man of foresight, whose judgment was proved correct by the event.

I should be neither better nor worse, but I should be treated as one who had the right to his country's gratitude. I prefer not to have been that man of foresight and judgment.

During the years of German occupation I endured many long hours when I was near to desperation. At times I uttered certain words or did certain acts. My purpose was always to avoid the necessity for far-reaching action, often to obviate the necessity for any action at all.

I constantly tried to ease our wounds, to break our chains, and to counter the perpetual German menace. More and more I made promises which I was determined not to keep. As against men like Hitler, Oberg, or Sauckel, I had no resources to draw upon except patience and tenacity of purpose. I had no forces at my command except my gift for negotiation and my power to persuade.[*]

* See, in this connection, Dr. Hans Richard Hemmen's (von Ribbentrop's representative in Paris) testimony given at Nürnberg on March 23rd, 1948, Appendix XIII.

I applied my whole intelligence in my country's service. I knew that my interlocutors had no faith except bad faith and that their methods were brutal and extreme. I mobilised all my wit, all my heart, and all my mind, matured by many years of political experience. I fought constantly day by day, and often night by night, to close some difficult negotiation, to reduce seizure of property, to prevent heartless requisitions, to forestall the departure of workmen, to return prisoners to their homes, to save poor creatures condemned to death.

I devoted every waking minute to saving France, to preserving its framework and its life. There were untold suffering, wounds which never will be healed, but this I could not prevent. I say in modest humility that I preserved in the body of France that breath of life which permitted her to survive, to be liberated and to begin her renaissance.

I did my best. That is all I claim. But who could have done better than I did when confronted by an enemy as harsh, as unprincipled, and as pitiless as the German was? Another man would have saved his honour, you may say. Yes, perhaps, if he had looked at things in a different light. And in doing so he would surely have crucified France.

I have a different concept of honour. I subordinate my personal honour to the honour of my country. My ideal of honour was to make every sacrifice in order to spare our country the final indignity of being ruled by a Gauleiter or by a band of adventurers, to avoid a declaration of war on the Anglo-Saxon powers and to obviate an alliance with the German Reich. I achieved my goal.

For me the road of honour consisted in lightening the burden of suffering and sorrow for the whole French people. Tens of thousands of men and women, Frenchmen and Frenchwomen, owe me their lives. Hundreds of thousands more can thank me for their freedom.

Note

The following pages on Europe's future and the atomic bomb were written by Pierre Laval on August 8, 1945. While he was writing them he learned in his prison cell that the first atomic bomb had been used. It was only a few days later that he began answering the charges brought against him.

AUGUST 8TH, 1945

In 1940 Germany and the Soviets were Allies. France was defeated and prostrate. She had to be prepared for a German victory and to organise her policy and her future accordingly. The fate of Europe was to be under German and Russian domination. We had little to fear. In future, we could lean toward Russia should German rule curtail our rights; for example, we could take advantage of our prestige in Central and Eastern Europe. Germany lost, and lost because she blundered twice: She failed to make peace with France, thus provoking American intervention, and she attacked Russia. Bismark once said that Germany could not wage and win a war on two fronts, east and west. She had a powerful army, wonderfully equipped, but a diplomacy which fell far short of her strength. She had, in fact, won the war but had never seized the opportunities to consolidate her position. Over-weaning pride and unbounded ambition were to cause her downfall and, perhaps, her dismemberment. As the Allies in Potsdam have just agreed to her unity, this last will not occur. She will therefore, from now on, be placed largely within the Soviet orbit and Europe will henceforth be under Russian domination. Many people believe that America, with the British, will oppose the extension of Soviet influence in western Europe. The United States, which have had to wage two wars, one as yet unfinished, will quickly tire and sooner or later inevitably withdraw their troops from Europe. At that moment, Great Britain will have neither the desire nor the strength to bar alone the way to Communism. Germany, with her regimentation, is politically ripe to receive the Soviet mark and it is unlikely that her old conservative parties, with their kings and princes, will be able to withstand the communistic pressure of German labor. One must therefore consider the establishment of Communism in Europe as an historical fact (a formidable and unexpected one for those who paved the way for it).

We have here an event of paramount importance and one which must give pause to those who are responsible for their countries' destinies. In reframing German unity, a decision I should personally have subscribed to, the Big Three have let Stalin win the game, which means that sooner or later he will win Germany to Communism. She will turn to it very quickly after the Allied occupation troops leave. In any case, we must consider as definitely within the Russian orbit all those countries now occupied by the Soviet army or her satellites. We have Tito in Jugoslavia. In Roumania, Jugoslavia and Bulgaria, the era of kings is definitely over and the reign of Communism has begun. Czecho-Slovakia is subordinate to Moscow and, as to Poland, she may as well be considered from now on a component part of the U.S.S.R. So goes the world when it is led by conservatives like Churchill and when Stalin has had the incredible luck to find a blood-thirsty maniac at the helm of Germany. Whether we like it or not, we must face it realistically. We are now entering a new phase in human history, in which the masses, led by active and disciplined minorities imbued with new socialistic ideas, become masters of their own destinies. Thus ends the rule of a selfish bourgeoisie, which was either unable or unwilling to make its own survival possible by granting labour certain advantages. I deplore war, its destructions, its sufferings, its ruins, but the revolution which follows in its wake is its natural consequence, as was foreseen by men like Lenin.

As I write this I hear the Americans have just made use of a bomb called 'atomic' which, though small, is said to have an overwhelming effect. The war with Japan will end quickly and future wars be made impossible because of the destructive effects of this weapon. We must wait a few days to be sure, but I admit I am not surprised. I believed the Germans, who boasted so much about it, possessed such a device for use at the last moment. The weapon did exist, but in American hands. Will they be able to keep the secret long? That is the question. Be that as it may, for the moment they are masters of the international situation, although that does not modify the political problems posed by the war in Europe. In 1936 I met Stapel, who was studying methods of de-magnetising magnetos, of decomposing lubricants and of setting fires at long range.

Stapel failed, as did those who believed they were on the verge of discovering Death Rays. But I always maintained, even at the risk of being laughed at, that the moment was near when there would be a discovery so terrible as to render war impossible. The Americans can take advantage of this device not only militarily but politically, so as to influence the world situation for a time. However, we must not anticipate but wait to know whether or not the discovery has the importance ascribed to it. Japan would have no choice but to sue for peace and the realisation of Stalin's dream might be delayed. In a few days we shall know the exact implications of this sensational discovery and the consequences to be expected from it. Bichelonne, at Sigmaringen, had spoken to me at great length about the use which could be made of 'heavy water,' and I remember what he said. What I now hear about the new bomb reminds me of that conversation.

Bichelonne had devoted some time to similar researches and that explains his arrest by the Germans at the beginning of the Occupation.

Man is an intelligent animal who, after having developed every comfort, finally discovers the surest means of destroying his achievements. Thus have most civilisations disappeared.

(The next day, August 9th, 1945, Pierre Laval began answering the charges brought against him.)

APPENDICES

APPENDIX I

ACT OF ACCUSATION

*Chapters dealing with specific charges in the Act
of Accusation are indicated at the beginning
of each paragraph.*

[*Chapter I.*]—The career of Laval, before the war, began in
the parties of the Left, who later repudiated him. He was
several times a Minister, twice Prime Minister, and his
personal fortunes followed the course of his political fortunes.

[*Chapter II.*]—Overthrown in January 1936 after the failure
of his plan to settle the Ethiopian crisis, he was animated
by a hatred of England, which he held responsible for his
downfall, and with a hatred of the French Parliament,
whose confidence he was unable to regain.

[*Chapter III.*]—From the outbreak of war he seems to have
taken it upon himself to negotiate for a peace, thanks to
the special relationship which he claimed to have with
Mussolini. At the same time, he sought to obtain Italy's
assistance in taking France out of the war and to endow
France with a political system similar to that which Mussolini had evolved for Italy.

[*Chapter IV.*]—When the military situation of May 1940
deteriorated, Laval was in the forefront of those who demanded an Armistice. Thus his name was included in the
list which Pétain presented to the President of the Republic immediately following the resignation of Paul Reynaud. For the time being he remained in the background,
but three weeks later he appeared in the vanguard, and

from that time forward he played a preponderant role throughout the period which preceded 10 July 1940.

[*Chapter V*.]—Without doubt he bears the greatest responsibility, as a result of his intrigues and of his threats which involved even the immediate entourage of the President of the Republic. The President of the Republic, the presidents of the two Chambers, the members of Parliament, and those ministers who still had any concern for the national sovereignty, failed to go to North Africa. In North Africa they might have formed a government removed from immediate threat of German reprisals which, before Europe and America, might suitably have represented France and affirmed the continuation of its sovereign role among the nations.

He it is who, by means of intrigue, political bargaining, promises, and threats, induced the Parliament to turn the Government of the Republic over to Marshal Pétain.

[*Chapter VI*.]—Thus the indictment of Laval on the charge of endangering the internal security of the State is fully justified. He himself confessed his guilt in this respect with unblushing pride when, in a speech to the schoolteachers of Mayet de Montagne, he said: 'You will grant that, under the general ægis of Marshal Pétain, I am responsible for the most important development of the national revolution, that is, the decree of 10 July 1940.'

It is he, moreover, who, as Vice-President of the Council of Ministers and political heir apparent of the Marshal, was the first to profit from the *coup d'état* of 11 July which suppressed the office of President of the Republic, concentrated all executive power in the person of Pétain, and brought about the dismissal of the Parliament *sine die*.

An absolutist regime, such as Laval's and Pétain's was, could have been established in France only with the connivance of the invader.

[*Chapter VII*.]—The Montoire meeting, which Laval engi-

neered, and the agreements which resulted from it and
which had as object a collaboration which made our resources and our means of existence available to the Germans was, in terms of foreign policy, in the enemy's interest, and must be classed under the heading of a crime in
the terms of Article 75 of the Penal Code.

[*Chapter VIII.*]—However, a palace revolution was soon to
bring about the downfall of Laval. This was preceded by
the brutal dismissal of Laval by Pétain. In fact, Pétain
ordered Laval's arrest.

[*Chapter IX.*]—Several weeks thereafter, the newspapers working for the Axis engaged in a violent campaign with the
object of forcing the Marshal to take back his former chief
of government. Laval permitted this campaign without
protesting. It required the anglo-phobia, the obsequious-
ness, and the treason of Darlan to calm the Reich pending
the return of its protégé, but the moment came when the
skilful manœuvring of Laval prevailed in the eyes of Germany over all the concessions which the Admiral was prepared to grant and Laval returned to power fortified by
the support of the occupying authorities.

[*Chapter X.*]—The so-called French policy thereupon became
a 100 per cent German policy: persecution of the Jews,
Freemasons, Communists, and of the Resistance in every
party. The police were placed at the disposal of the
Gestapo. In the night of 15-16 July there were 22,000
arrests in Paris alone.

[*Chapter XI.*]—It was his hope that France would aid Germany on a military basis. But because he lacked the arms
which the Germans, fearing not him but the French people, dared not furnish, he undertook to replace in the
factories in Germany the workmen whom Hitler had
mobilised.

On 22 June he revealed his hand once more when he
appealed to the French workers to go to Germany on the

pretext that this would free to France agricultural workers from the concentration camps in Germany, according to a promise of Hitler for which he was publicly thanked by Laval. The men of our fields and the men of our factories must display a mutual loyalty, Laval continued. The wife whose husband could thus return would be for ever grateful to the unknown workman who, by sacrificing himself and going to Germany, had permitted the return of her husband from a prison camp.

Despite his appeals, volunteers for work in Germany were not forthcoming and Laval was obliged to resort to force. First in order came a law governing the use of industrial man-power which, in fact, subordinated men and women workers to the will of the Government, which could thenceforth decide where and how they were to work. Next came a law preventing employers from enlisting workers without a formal authorisation of the Government so that the number of unemployed should be reduced and in consequence there would be fewer volunteers for work in Germany. Then came the law making work obligatory, which was a cover for virtual conscription and veritable slave markets for workers to be delivered to the Reich, with all the consequent measures such as refusals of food cards, organised man-hunts and the whole series of measures which were recommended to the Prefects in a stream of instructions.

[*Chapter XII.*]—Abandoning all discretion, Laval, on 22 June 1942, challenged the French people with his notorious statement: 'I foresee a German victory.'

At Compiègne, in August 1942, he explained his purpose when he said that the momentous and victorious struggle which Germany had undertaken had need of all its man-power. As a consequence, it required workers.

Thus began the thievery of the so-called change of guards of the relief, which Laval himself confirmed was thievery when, after stressing the need of the Reich for workers, he said: 'As for the release of our war prisoners, their day will come on that day when a German victory is consummated.'

[*Chapter XIII*.]—Laval and Pétain made an open alliance with the Axis against the Anglo-Americans and the French Forces in Morocco and Algeria, but in vain. The armies of the Axis were routed. Bizerta was opened to them but they had to evacuate Tunis simultaneously with the defeat of the Italian army in Libya. The defeat of Germany loomed as a certainty. Hope began to dawn in France. At this the fury of Laval knew no limits.

[*Chapter XIV*.]—Laval and Pétain preferred to see the fleet destroyed; it lurked at Toulon, rather than play the military role which would have been to the profit of France and of her allies.

On the other hand, the insistence of Laval in obtaining from Admiral Robert in the Antilles the sinking of the fleet and the burning of the aeroplanes, through fear that the Americans might make use of them, throws new light on the sentiments of a Government which preferred to see our warships destroyed rather than allow them to contribute to our liberation.

[*Chapter XV*.]—The revelation, showing the brutality with which, after July 1940 and in violation of the Armistice, the Germans began the annexation of Alsace-Lorraine, shows how odious Laval's Montoire policy was, particularly in so far as the people of Alsace-Lorraine were concerned.

Did Laval not accept this situation with complete indifference and as a *fait accompli* in his message to the American people of 25 May 1941?

[*Chapter XVII*.]—As a consequence of this policy, France suffered a moral and material detriment which, in spite of her great sacrifices and her material contribution to victory, she is still bearing.

This is justly a crime of which the man is guilty who, shielded under the banner of Pétain, was the original instigator of collaboration. We truly say that had it not been for the martyrdom and heroism of the great majority of Frenchmen, many of whom gave their lives, this would have been active, and it would have marked with an indelible blot the saddest page in our history.

Political treason, moral treason, betrayal of France to the invader—these are the conclusions which must be drawn from this Act of Accusation, which is merely a chronological table of events known to all.

Pending his appearance in court, documents, testimony, and later—history, will prove the guilt of Laval. This is proved sufficiently now to justify calling him before the High Court.

APPENDIX II

THE pages you are about to read are in no sense Memoirs. My father thought too much in terms of State Affairs and State secrets to write his own history. You, the British, need no explanation of the significance of such words. If he had retired from public life, and had reached old age, he might perhaps have written his reminiscences; I hardly believe so. I think that my father would never have been old or retired.

These pages were written in a prison cell crawling with vermin where, deprived of all documents, he had to rely upon his memory alone. The Provisional Government of 1944-1945 had seized all his papers. 'Must France then remain ignorant of her history?' were among the last words my father wrote immediately before his death.

The following notes were destined to serve during his trial, which culminated in the judicial scandal known to all, and were written on sheets of paper handed to me by his attorneys, so that I might have them typed and returned to him for correction. This is how the manuscript of this book was pieced together. It contains the replies to every count of the Act of Accusation. I believe that it should interest you. Among other things you will find a chapter dealing with my father's relations with Great Britain. It had been asserted that Pierre Laval was one of England's enemies. That is for you to judge, but let me comment briefly upon this chapter.

Strange as it may seem, I, who love my father and whose admiration for him is unbounded, believe that once in his life he might have been accused of high treason; this was in 1931 and for your country's sake. In point of fact, as Prime Minister of the Third French Republic, he decided, without consulting either his ministers, the Chamber of Deputies, or the Senate, to place at the disposal of Great Britain all the financial resources of his country.

On 19th September 1931, at about one o'clock in the morning, he was awakened by a telephone call from your Chargé d'Affaires, Sir Ronald Campbell. (Ambassador Tyrrell had been summoned home, some days earlier, to confer with his Government.)

My father thought at first that it must be some joke, for in those days it was not a British diplomatic custom to work at night—even week-ends were sacred.

He speedily recognised the voice of Sir Ronald, who sounded eager and anxious.

'M. le Président, I am calling you to request an urgent meeting.'

My father suggested the same morning at eight. Sir Ronald, embarrassed, replied:

'M. le Président, would it not be possible to see you immediately? The matter is grave and pressing.'

'Certainly, come at once,' answered my father and he began to dress.

Sir Ronald arrived a few minutes later at the Home Office, Place Beauvau.

'I am directed by my Government to ask your help and advice,' Sir Ronald said.

He then disclosed the tragic situation of the Bank of England following the enormous withdrawals of gold, and the impossibility of the Government's meeting its financial obligations if immediate aid were not given.

My father replied: 'To-morrow morning I shall call a Cabinet meeting to take up the question.'

Sir Ronald responded: 'M. le Président, the matter is much too grave and too secret for twelve Cabinet members to be informed of it. The slightest indiscretion would cause irreparable damage to Great Britain's prestige; moreover, the urgency is extreme.'

Sir Ronald then handed my father the memorandum which he had written for the French Minister of Finance

and which your representative had been instructed by telephone to communicate to no one but the Prime Minister.
You will find in an appendix to this book the photographic
facsimile of this document with the French translation which
Sir Ronald himself wrote, as he did not wish to confide the
secret to his colleagues at the Embassy.*

Deeply moved by the position in which your country found
itself and appreciating Sir Ronald's attitude of grave dignity,
my father continued: 'You ask my advice. Here it is. Let your
Government determine the amount of the credit which is
necessary. Get in touch immediately with Washington and
ask the United States to subscribe one-half of the necessary
amount while pointing out that France has already agreed
as far as her own half is concerned. Personally, I don't believe
that the United States will be in a position to agree to this,
so come back to-morrow morning and if the United States
do not agree to participate I will renew my offer, but for the
entire credit.' My father added: *Dans ce cas, j'ouvre tout
grands les coffres de mon pays.'* ('In that case I will open
wide the coffers of my country.') Two tears ran down Sir
Ronald's cheeks as he clasped both my father's hands and
said: 'M. le Président, I thank you. My country will never
forget. . . .'

The following morning he returned to the Place Beauvau
to say that the United States had made known that it was
impossible for them to come to the aid of Great Britain. You
will see in the appendix to this book the facsimile of the
second memorandum Sir Ronald wrote and which he gave
my father that day.** My father then confirmed his offer of
the previous night. That is how the three-thousand-million-
franc credit was made to your country, a credit that allowed
Great Britain to devaluate her currency a few days later in
a manner which astonished the world.

Was my father justified in taking on himself this decision,

* Appendix II, (a), (b) and (c).

** Appendix II, (d) and (e).

which might have had far-reaching consequences upon the finances of his own country? It is true that we were rich then, as France always was under the governments over which he presided.

Four years later, in 1935, at the time of the Abyssinian war, your Government decided to send the Home Fleet to the Mediterranean. Some months earlier my father had negotiated and signed a military pact with Italy in order to prevent the annexation of Austria by Hitler. He considered that an alliance with Italy was indispensable to the maintenance of peace in Europe. But Italy was Fascist and part of your public opinion opposed the signing of this treaty.

I will give you my father's opinion on this subject. He believed that each individual has the right to hold the convictions which his conscience dictates, but that a statesman has not the right to impose his personal opinion when his country must face certain geographical realities and political necessities. A statesman may find himself constrained to negotiate with a foreign government of which he disapproves. Governments and regimes pass away but countries and their peoples remain.

It was in October 1935 that your Ambassador, Sir George Clark, called upon my father, who was then Prime Minister and Minister of Foreign Affairs, and informed him of the passage of the Home Fleet through the Straits of Gibraltar. He pointed out that the fleet would not be able to sustain unaided the weight of combat if attacked by Italy and he inquired what attitude France would take in the event that the application of sanctions by Great Britain brought about a state of war in the Mediterranean. There was at that time no treaty of alliance between France and Great Britain. Indeed some months earlier, the British Government, without the knowledge of France, had signed a naval pact with Germany.

Nevertheless, my father telephoned our Ambassador in Rome, my uncle, Charles de Chambrun, and instructed him

to inform Mussolini at once that if Italy attacked the British
Fleet, our army, our navy, and our air force would immediately take sides with Great Britain.

As on the previous occasion which I have just recalled,
this decision had to be taken by my father alone without
consulting the Council of Ministers, the House of Representatives, or the Senate.

More scrupulous than many in regard to State secrets he
never spoke publicly of these events, which I relate here for
the first time, and this is why they have until now remained
unknown to you.

Do you wish to know what one of your greatest Ambassadors thought of my father? This is what Lord Tyrrell wrote
to me on 19th July 1935 on the occasion of my marriage,
and in the midst of the Abyssinian crisis:

> 'Will you kindly remember me to your parents, who
> were always so kind to me during my stay in Paris, a
> kindness and friendship which I value very highly and
> shall never forget. It was such a joy to me if at any party
> I discovered the friendly smile of your charming mother.
> As for your father, I am lost in admiration for the magnificent courage and statesmanship he is showing in the present crisis.'

Thus, twice in the course of his career and in circumstances of extreme gravity, my father adopted towards Great
Britain the attitude which I have just described. In so doing
he had always in mind the higher interests of his country
and of world peace.

When the storm later descended upon us and our country
was occupied, he again took the attitude which seemed to
him, at that time, most consistent with the interests of
France. His great concern was to relieve the everyday sufferings of the greatest possible number of Frenchmen, through
long and difficult daily negotiations with the occupying
power.

The pages you will read are but the account of those years when, guided alone by his courage, tenacity, and patriotism, my father—receiver for a bankruptcy he had done everything to avert—struggled to assure France a modicum of existence under circumstances which grew daily more difficult. It was no longer a question of the France represented by the handful of men who could still fight at your side, nor of the France which had taken refuge in America, but of that France which was under German occupation.

JOSÉE de CHAMBRUN

Sir Ronald Campbell's Memorandum to Pierre Laval
18 September 1931

BRITISH EMBASSY,
PARIS.

le 18 Septembre

Monsieur le Président,

Veuillez trouver, ci-inclus, la traduction du message du chancelier de l'Échiquier. Vu le caractère du document je n'ai pas pu recourir aux experts pour les termes techniques. J'espère néanmoins que le sens sera clair.

Agréez, Monsieur le Président, l'assurance de ma haute considération et de mes sentiments les meilleurs.

R. H. Campbell

The British Embassy,
PARIS.   18 September.

MONSIEUR LE PRÉSIDENT,

Please find enclosed the translation of the message of the Chancellor of the Exchequer. Because of the character of the document I have not been able to resort to experts for the translation of the technical terms. I hope nevertheless the meaning will be clear to you.

Please accept, Monsieur le Président, the assurance of my high esteem and of my kind regards.

APPENDIX III (b)

Sir Ronald Campbell's Memorandum, 19 September 1931

BRITISH EMBASSY,
PARIS.

Personnel. Très

Sécret.

En raison des demandes
exceptionnelles sur les crédits du
gouvernement britannique je tiens à
vous faire connaître instamment la
situation.

Y compris les engagements
acceptés nous avons épuisé £ 50,000,000
sur les £ 80,000,000 (crédits de) obtenus au début de
ce mois. Le rythme des tirages s'est
accéléré. Le 16 septembre nous avons
utilisé £ 5,000,000 et le 17 septembre près
de £ 7,500,000. Les demandes du continent
autrement que de la France ont continué

et

192

BRITISH EMBASSY,
PARIS.

et accroissent rapidement à mesure que
la situation à Amsterdam empire. En
outre Amsterdam a retiré jusq'à midi
£ 2,000,000 En or de la Banque d'Angleterre.
Les Banques anglaises n'ont aucun indice
de retraits considérables par des
nationaux britanniques et attribuent le
mouvement En tout premier lieu à la
nervosité d'autres Centres quant à la
liquidité de leur situation.

    Le Gouvernement britannique
à réussi à équilibrer le budget et a
obtenu une majorité au parlement pour
mettre En Exécution leur politique de
redressement, y compris la diminution
de l'assistance aux chômeurs. Ils Sont
               En

BRITISH EMBASSY,
PARIS.

En voie d'imposer de nouvels impôts
draconiens. Ceci a fait beaucoup pour
rétablir la confiance dans notre
situation, mais, à la suite de
développements pour lesquels nous ne
sommes pas responsables, les retraits
de Londres ont recommencé depuis et
vont toujours accroissant. Quand les
crédits actuellement disponibles seront
épuisés nous aurons supporté des
demandes sur nos réserves en or
et en devises remontant à plus de
£ 200,000,000 en deux mois sans
compter plus de £ 70,000,000 immobilisés
en Allemagne. Selon le rythme actuel
                                        le

4

BRITISH EMBASSY,
PARIS.

le Solde encore disponible de nos Crédits sera épuisé dans très peu de jours et en l'absence d'autres Crédits le gouvernement se verra avec regret obligé de suspendre les paiements en or. Le résultat n'en serait pas borné à ce pays mais aurait des répercussions internationales très étendues. Nos banquiers prévoient qu'il serait extrêmement difficile d'obtenir d'autres Crédits banquiers de l'importance nécessaire. Dans ces conditions je crois devoir vous faire connaître en confiance la situation pour le cas où votre gouvernement pourrait venir en aide. Il n'est pas nécessaire d'ajouter que l'affaire est d'une extrême urgente.

APPENDIX III (c)

TRANSLATION OF THE MEMORANDUM OF 19 SEPTEMBER 1931

PARIS.

Personal and very Secret.

"In view of the quite
Exceptional drain on the Credits to the
British Government I feel that "you
should know of the position immediately.

Including Commitments we
have Exhausted fifty million pounds
(£50,000,000) out of the eighty million pounds
(£80,000,000) Credit raised at the beginning
of this month. The rate of withdrawal
has recently been accelerating. On September
16th we lost £5,000,000 and on Sept 17th
£7,500,000. The drain from the Continent

other

2

BRITISH EMBASSY,
PARIS.

other than France has been continued
and is increasing rapidly as trouble in
Amsterdam develops. Amsterdam in
addition has taken up to noon two
million pounds (£2.000.000) in gold from
the Bank of England. English Banks
have no evidence of any substantial
withdrawals by British nationals and
ascribe the movement predominantly to
nervousness in other centres as regards
the liquidity of their position.

　　　　The Government here have
successfully balanced the budget and
have obtained a majority in Parliament
for carrying out a policy of retrenchment
including a cut in unemployment
　　　　　　　　　　expenditure

3.

BRITISH EMBASSY,
PARIS.

Expenditure, and will be imposing drastic
taxation. This had a marked effect
in restoring Confidence in our position
but as a result of developments
abroad for which we are not responsible
withdrawals from London have since been
resumed in increasing volume. Present
credits are exhausted we shall have stood
a drain of a loss of gold and to our
own foreign Exchange reserve of over
£ 200,000,000 in two months apart
from the optional £ 70,000,000 frozen in
Germany.

At the present rate of
withdrawal the unused balance of
credits will be used in a very few
days

4

BRITISH EMBASSY,
PARIS.

days and in the absence of further
credits the no alternative but Government reluctantly will
have to suspend gold payments. The
effect of this could not be limited to
this country but must be far-reaching
internationally. Our Bankers anticipate
that it would be a matter of
extreme difficulty to secure further
banking credits of the very large amount
that would be required. In these
circumstances I think that it is only
right to inform you in confidence
of the position in case you. Gov.t can
help. It is scarcely necessary to add
that matter is one of extreme urgency.

APPENDIX III (d)

TEXT OF SIR RONALD CAMPBELL'S LETTER TO PIERRE LAVAL
19 SEPTEMBER 1931

le 19 septembre.

BRITISH EMBASSY,
PARIS.

Monsieur le Président

Voici le résumé de ce que j'ai
eu la charge de porter ce soir a votre
connaissance

D'après un télégramme de
Washington le gouvernement des Etats
Unis se trouve dans l'impossibilité de
venir en aide au gouvernement britannique.
Il ne saurait plus être question de
Crédits bancaires. Vu ses obligations existentes
le "Federal Reserve Board" n'y peut rien.
Le Président ne possède pas le pouvoir de
prêter les fonds publics sans le consentement
du Congrès. Convoquer le Congrès en session
spéciale entraînerait des débats prolongés

200

2

BRITISH EMBASSY,
PARIS.

Sans Certitude quant au résultat.

Dans Ces Conditions le
Gouvernement britannique se voit obligé
de mettre en exécution les mesures
prévues dans le message du Chancelier de
l'Echiquier, et l'action parlementaire que
Comporte la situation sera prise dès
lundi même.

Je Suis Chargé En même
temps de vous exprimer M. le Président
les remerciements très sincères du
Gouvernement britannique pour la très
amicale manière dont vous avez
accueilli son appel, et qui est
hautement appréciée. Le doute que vous
aviez exprimé quant à l'efficacité de
n'importe quel expédient à l'heure

3.

BRITISH EMBASSY,
PARIS

actuelle se trouve pleinement
confirmé par le fait que le
montant des achats dans les
derniers quatre jours est de £ 40,000,000,
soit cinq milliards de francs.

Veuillez agréer M. le Président
l'assurance de ma haute considération
et de mes sentiments les meilleurs.

R. W. Campbell

APPENDIX III (e)

The British Embassy,
PARIS.   19 September.

MONSIEUR LE PRÉSIDENT,

Please find herewith the summary which it is my duty to bring to your knowledge.

According to a telegram just received from Washington, the United States Government finds it impossible to go to the aid of the British Government. It can no longer be a question of bank credits. Because of existing obligations the Federal Reserve Board is powerless. The President has no power to loan public funds without the permission of Congress.

The British Government is therefore obliged to execute the measures announced by the Chancellor of the Exchequer and this political action will be taken on Monday next. I am requested at the same time to express to you, Monsieur le Président, the very sincere gratitude of the British Government for the extremely friendly way in which you have answered this appeal, which is highly appreciated. The doubt which you expressed as to the possibility of any other solution at the present time is completely confirmed by the fact that the withdrawals in the past four days amount to £40,000,000—that is to say, five billion francs.

Please accept, Monsieur le Président, the assurance of my high esteem and of my kind regards.

APPENDIX IV

Address of Pierre Laval to the Mayors of Cantal, at Vichy, November 9th, 1943

During the occupation years the Governors, mayors, magistrates and higher executives were in the habit of coming to Vichy or the Hotel Matignon to see the Marshal or my father in order to inform and document themselves. They felt the need of guidance in the midst of the contradictory and sometimes excessive propaganda which saturated France. My father always received them and often talked freely with them when he felt he could do so in confidence.

In order to avoid leaks, his words were not supposed to be taken down, but most of them were transcribed by a reliable secretary without his knowledge.

Later, I shall publish a collection of these speeches and therefore, in order not to overload this book, only one, which seems to me especially interesting, is here included.

J. L. de C.

I am much touched by the words I have just heard. I have often received delegations coming here from all over France, but nothing could warm my heart more than the speech of the President of the Council of the Department of Cantal.

I come, as do you all, from Auvergne. That is to say that I am a Frenchman through and through. No-one from our section can help loving his country passionately.

Certainly I did not want war. I have too great a share of our good peasant sense to have wished for war.

A country must wage war when it has been attacked and has the right and duty to wage it in self-defence. That was often the case with France. It was true in 1914 but in 1939 we were not attacked.

A country may also wage war when it is hungry, in order
to eat, but that was not our case. France was contented and
prosperous, perhaps too much so, and failed to appreciate
her good fortune.

A country may wage war to defend its honour, but our
honour was not at stake in 1939. We did not fight when
Germany annexed Austria. We did not declare war when she
re-militarised the Rhineland. Neither did we do so when
she took over Czecho-Slovakia.

We went to war for the Danzig Corridor. Today the
whole world, the diplomatists of every nation, acknowledge
that the Danzig Corridor was a piece of crude bungling,
the worst, perhaps, in the entire Versailles treaty. One can
always divide a country in two pieces by force, and there
was Germany on one side and East Prussia beyond, but,
knowing the history of mankind, it is inconceivable that a
country, having regained its strength, should accept such a
situation. At Geneva, the representatives of all the nations,
even those most hostile to Germany, agreed that an amicable
solution to this difficult problem had to be found. Yet it
was for the Danzig Corridor that France went to war.

Many said we went to war 'because of our obligations to
Poland'. Today I am speaking to men of Auvergne and I
know you will understand me correctly. Were it true that
we were bound by treaty with Poland to declare war, the
boldest might say to me, 'Even at the risk of defeat, it was
a question of our honour; we had to fight'. Well, I shall prove
that false, because we were not obliged to go to war for
Poland.

I was the colleague and friend of Aristide Briand. He
signed in 1925 the Treaty of Locarno, which guaranteed the
eastern frontiers of France. This guarantee was subscribed to
by England and Italy also. On the same day, Briand signed
a treaty with Czecho-Slovakia and another with Poland and,
while the Franco-Soviet and Franco-Polish treaties were not
included in the Locarno pact, they were published the same
day and in the same issue of the 'Journal Officiel'. They

were interconnected and I frequently heard Briand, in 1925 (Painleve was then Prime Minister), report on his negotiations and the results he had obtained. He told us that the engagements he had entered into with Poland and Czecho-Slovakia were but the logical and natural results of those made by England and Italy regarding France's eastern frontiers. The treaties with Poland, signed by Millerand in 1921 and 1922, were annulled and superceded by the treaty of 1925.

At the time of the re-militarisation of the left bank of the Rhine, when England refused to apply against Germany the clauses in the Locarno pact, France's guarantee to Poland automatically lapsed. It was said or rumoured that we had made other pledges to Poland, in addition to those in the treaty of 1925. There were said to be secret military agreements. Well, I can ask you, you who represent the good common-sense of our regions, such military agreements could hardly be kept secret from the Prime Minister, could they? Now in 1931, 1932, and 1935 I was Head of the Government. Military agreements could scarcely remain a secret from the Minister of Foreign Affairs in 1932 and 1935, and I can tell you to-day they were so secret that I never heard about them. (Sensation.)

I am telling this to you, my compatriots from Cantal, and some day, when at last I shall be able to speak freely, I shall tell it to the world without fear of contradiction.

I will go further. In 1939, when the Daladier Government drew up the military budget, I felt a black forboding that we should be drawn into the war if we voted for those credits.

I had no desire to refuse any military credits. Throughout my public life I have never refused credits for military purposes, because they were necessary and indispensable for France. There was no question of refusing the credits, when I asked to speak that day. One or two of you probably attended that session. Those who did will remember it. I was greeted by the vociferations of those who had for years, consistently, refused to arm France and some of whom are now at Algiers, expressing themselves so unjustly towards the man who, after all, is only the assignee of their bankruptcy.

What does our Constitution say? One thing which to me was vital and sacred: France cannot and should not declare war without the consent of Parliament. Neither the Senate nor the Chamber of Deputies were ever called upon to vote either for or against war. You Republicans, who respect legal procedure, never forget what I have just told you: we went into this war illegally.

Had we had a secret session what should I have told the Senators? I should have told them, only in greater detail, for I should have had the time to speak slowly and at length, just what I have told you. And I should have added something more; I should have said: 'We are going to war alone and we cannot win'. Then the Auvergnat in me would have continued and said: 'Does one go to war alone, in the certainty that France will have to pay with tragic suffering for her imprudence?' No—is not that the answer?

Well, I should have said then that we were going to fight without modern bombing planes. I should have added, incorrectly, that we had only nine modern bombers. The truth, which I learned later, was that we had none and that the nine I referred to were not received until two months after hostilities had begun, whereas Germany had three thousand modern bombers.

Germany and Russia had just divided Poland between them. We entered the war practically alone and lost it. Why? Because this war is not like the others, it is not in defence of the land of our fathers. It is not a war to defend our country. It is a war of passionate fanaticism, in which ideologies contend against each other.

I am speaking in an ancient land of Freedom, lost momentarily but soon, I hope, to be regained, and I affirm that we went into this war for ideas which are not our own.

If Russia has communism at home, that is her affair, but let her keep her communism there. (Applause.)

If Germany has National-Socialism at home, that is her affair, but let her keep her National-Socialism there. (Applause.)

If America and Great Britain cherish anti-fascist ideologies, that is their affair. But we of Auvergne, who are ignorant of fascism, who have never suffered the imprint of any race other than that of our own ancient province, no one can force us to accept those ideologies. We went to war, and our young men left, for the sake of ideologies and not to defend the Juy-de-Dôme and the meadows of our Cantal.

All my life, you know it, you do, I have been an apostle of peace. I have been mayor, deputy, senator and minister often: Socialist I have always been and still am to the depths of my heart. The Marshal once said that our proletarian conditions must be eradicated. How right he is! I have often been slandered and abused but always felt that when I was being most slandered and abused I was best fulfilling my duty to France. I have known painful moments when some of those within the labouring classes, who had given me their esteem and friendship, were being robbed of that esteem and friendship because I would not subscribe to the schemes of those who were lying to them every day, who deceived them and who, after disarming them, were leading them straight into war.

Women bear children, fathers struggle to raise them and then, one day, a few politicians without conscience throw them into the crucible. That is why I hate war. It never pays; even France, as has been proven, when she wins a war has much to suffer.

Now then, what is happening? Every morning, every day, every Frenchman listens to the radio and hears the dispatches. We do not like Germany here, especially not in Auvergne. Our education has not been in that direction. Most of our battles have been fought against her.

However, life is hard and the history of mankind is complex. The fact is that today, were Germany to be suddenly eliminated, believe me and remember what I am saying (for

I ask you to remember every statement, as you did what I told you before), chaos will little by little establish itself in Europe. It will establish itself in Germany, in the Balkans, in Italy. Now I love my village, I love every stone at home, but I do not want disorder to install itself there. I want to act in such a way that Germany will not be strong enough to crush us, so that Bolshevism may not suppress us. Do you understand me correctly? That is the tragedy I live each day. Only yesterday I was in Paris and talked with the Germans until late into the night. They were not easy, those talks. They never are. You see, each day I try to do the maximum, in order that we may have to endure only the minimum in damages, and when night falls I often have the impression of being caught in a pair of pincers and wonder sadly which one, the German or the French, has caused me most suffering that day. Nevertheless, I never lose courage, for I have but one ambition, one goal, and only one, toward which I strive like a sort of sleepwalker: to try to do everything to save our country by reducing her sufferings each day, to act so that the land of our fathers shall remain in the hands of their children and so that that land may always be called the land of France. (Long applause.)

Now, you who are men of common-sense, you who represent the pioneers among Frenchmen, because you come from the summits of our land, because you represent ancient Gaul, whence came the cries of hope and the salvation of our country, I ask you, even though you may not always understand me (since we are not free and I do not like to talk—as a matter of fact, I do not know why I gave you so much of my confidence today)—Well! whenever you are in your villages I ask you to tell yourselves, no matter what happens or whatever I do, that I shall always be doing it because I believe it is the way to try to rescue our country, to assure peace and to save the civilisation into which we were born and in which we shall continue to live. (Lengthy ovation. The mayors rise and cheer.)

APPENDIX V

NOTE

The photostat here reproduced, together with a translation, is the report made by Sauckel to Hitler on the subject of forced labour in France.

To this report is attached the telegram sent by the head of the Gestapo in Vichy setting forth the information which had just been communicated to him by de Brinon after the secret meeting of the members of the Cabinet held in Vichy on the same day, the purpose of which was to deal with the question of forced labour. Both documents are from the German archives in Berlin. They were withdrawn from the files of the Prosecution at the de Brinon trial as being too favourable to Pierre Laval and Marshal Pétain.

> G.Z. 5780/366/43G.
> Secret Reich business.
> Paris, 9 August 1943

MY FÜHRER,

I feel it my duty to make the following report to you on the course so far taken in the effort to obtain the maximum recruitment of French labour for the benefit of the German war economy in France and in the Reich.

In view of the extremely urgent requirements in labour recruitment the purpose of my official conferences in France has been:

1. In France itself, to transfer, by the end of this year, one million French workmen and working-women from the French civilian manufacturing industry to manufacturing for the German armament industry in France;

210

2. Down to the end of this year, to import 100,000 French workers—men and women—monthly into the Reich armament industry; and

3. In France itself, in order to carry out these greatly increased and ever more urgent tasks, to develop and accelerate the labour recruitment organisation in such a manner that it shall be able to attain its objective in spite of the passive resistance of the French authorities.

The Military Commander, the Services of the Reich Minister for Armaments and Munitions, Party Comrade Speer, the departments of the S.S. Reichsführer, and the German Embassy were fully informed of these necessities. They were all entirely in accord with the projected measures and have promised their active assistance. After full agreement had been established among all these German departments, these requirements of the German labour recruitment were discussed in great detail, and very thoroughly, at the German Embassy with the French Prime Minister, who was accompanied by M. Bichelonne, Minister for Production; M. Bousquet, Secretary-General; and Ambassador de Brinon, Secretary of State.

The French Prime Minister, Laval, in fact attempted to have removed, in the future, the German supervisors of French factories working for German armament. This was flatly refused. The clear-cut demand of the General Plenipotentiary for recruitment of labour was maintained unconditionally. In the same way, the formation of German Labour Commissions in the French departments was also agreed to.

The French Prime Minister obstinately refused to carry out a further programme for recruiting and placing under contract the 500,000 French workers who were to go to Germany before the end of the year 1943. The negotiations dragged on for more than six hours. The French Prime Minister was unable to put forward any really sound reasons for his refusal. He stated that even my proposal that he should at least pledge himself to make the greatest efforts in an attempt to attain this objective was impossible of realisation. All his efforts appeared to be bent towards gaining political advantages for France. One argument which he kept putting forward anew was the danger of possible domestic political unrest in France if the workers designated for conscription should withdraw into the mountains and forests and carry on operations there as terrorists. Laval himself has obviously no longer sufficient authority to ensure that governmental bodies and the police shall be permanently and fully prepared at all times to carry out his measures. To a certain extent, however, this is Laval's own fault, for he has himself been very lax in seeing that the laws issued by him were executed and has even, in fact, not applied them at all. To this must be added that Laval has now completely isolated himself from such groups as, for instance, those of Doriot and Buchard, and has even quarrelled with them. At one time he even wanted to have them dissolved. The groups involved, however, are groups which have unreservedly proclaimed collaboration with Germany and supply the great majority of the contingents among the French volunteers, such as, for instance, for the S.S., the French Volunteers' Legion, the Todt Organisation, etc., and also openly support the German man-power recruitment. Laval's scarcely veiled refusal to send further strong contingents of workers to Germany under contract places German labour recruitment for the Reich in a very difficult position with respect to carrying out its tasks. It is no longer possible to avoid the suspicion that Laval is taking advantage of these difficulties because he, like everyone else in this country, appears completely to misunderstand the military and domestic situation of the Reich. Some allusions made by him make it clear that he believes he can now substitute France in Italy's place. For these reasons I have found it necessary to write the following letter to the German Representative and Minister, Party Member Schleier:

- 3 -   G.Z.: 5780/366/43 geh.Reiches.

lnneren Gesetze sehr lix wahrgenommen hat, ja zum Teil so-
gar nicht zur Anwendung brachte. Dazu kommt, dass jetzt Laval
sich auch von jenen Gruppen wie z.B. jener von Doriot und Bucard
vollkommen isoliert, ja verfeindet hat. Er wünschte einmal so-
gar deren Auflösung. Es handelt sich hier aber um Gruppen,
die vorbehaltlos die Zusammenarbeit mit Deutschland prokla-
miert haben und die die wesentlichsten Kontingente für die
französischen Freiwilligen , wie z.B. für die SS, für die französische Freiwilligenlegion, für die OT. usw. stellen und auch
den deutschen Arbeitseinsatz offen unterstützen. Die ziemlich
unverhüllte Ablehnung Lavals, weitere starke Arbeiterkontingen-
te nach Deutschland zu verpflichten, bringt aber den deutschen
Arbeitseinsatz im Reich hinsichtlich der Erfüllung seiner Auf-
gaben in eine sehr schwere Bedrängnis. Man kann sich nicht mehr
unbedingt von dem Verdacht frei machen, dass Laval diese Bedrängnis auslöst, weil auch er, wie es hierzulande allgemein
der Fall zu sein scheint, die militärische und innere Lage des
Reiches total verkennt. Zumindest lassen Anspielungen von ihm
erkennen, dass er glaubt, Frankreich jetzt an die Stelle Italiens
bringen zu können. Ich habe mich deshalb genötigt gesehen, an
den deutschen Geschäftsträger und Gesandten Pg. Schleier fol-
gendes Schreiben zu richten:

     "Sehr geehrter und lieber Pg. Schleier !

     Die mir durch Ihre Güte übermittelte Antwort des fran-
zösischen Ministerpräsidenten Laval habe ich immer wieder durch-
gelesen. Ebenso habe ich versucht, Ihre eigenen Ausführungen
die Sie heute Nachmittag bei mir machten als eine Rechtferti-
gung der Absage der französischen Regierung zu Punkt 3 (500 000
neue französische Arbeiter für Deutschland) innerlich anzuneh-
men.

     Nach ruhiger und kühler Überlegung muss ich Ihnen mit-
teilen, dass ich den Glauben an den ehrlichen und guten Willen
des französischen Ministerpräsidenten Laval vollkommen verlo-
ren habe. Seine Absage bedeutet eine glatte Sabotage des deut-

%/

Doc HAA 021

Sauckel's report to Hitler, August 9, 1943.
(Photostat of a page of the original.)

DEAR PARTY COMRADE SCHLEIER,

I have read over and over again the reply of the French Prime Minister, M. Laval, which you have been good enough to transmit to me. I have also endeavoured to absorb in my own mind the explanations which you yourself gave me this afternoon in justification of the French Government's refusal under Point 5 (500,000 new French workers for Germany).

After thinking the matter over calmly and coolly I must inform you that I have completely lost all faith in the honest goodwill of the French Prime Minister, Laval. His refusal amounts to pure and simple sabotage of Germany's struggle for life against Bolshevism. Moreover, this time again he personally made the worst imaginable impression, especially at the end of the negotiations, with his completely unjustified and confused statements in response to my clear and precise questions.

I would ask you to make it quite clear to him that an immediate revision of his obstinate refusal, before I leave, is his sole possibility for effacing this bad impression, for I shall inform the Führer of the complete truth regarding his present methods.

Nor has it escaped me that the French Ambassador, de Brinon, has been most painfully impressed by the attitude of his Prime Minister.

Heil Hitler!
Yours (*signed*) FRITZ SAUCKEL.

Notwithstanding the difficulties raised by the French, I shall now proceed, with the greatest energy and speed, to develop the projected efficient organisation for recruitment of labour in France, and endeavour on my own initiative to obtain the necessary workers for Germany in the field of labour recruitment in France. For, in fact, it is beyond all doubt that France still has extraordinary labour reserves both for labour recruitment for German purposes in France itself and also for employment in the Reich. The French Prime

Minister, Laval, has implicitly admitted this in the presence of his colleagues.

I am now being constantly reminded by all German departments of the necessity of once again giving German authority in France full force and effect. I have been informed by all the German departments and services that for this purpose the occupation of France by far greater numbers of German troops than is at present the case would be necessary. It would already be of the greatest assistance if a still larger number of training units were set up in the French territories with the greatest dispatch. Motorised units, in particular, are mentioned as being necessary.

As an illustration of the manœuvres of Laval, who appears to have acquiesced completely in Pétain demands, I attach hereunder:

1. The text of a dispatch from Vichy which has been sent to me by S.S. Standartenführer Dr. Knochen in his capacity as Director of the Security Department, and
2. Laval's official answer, as a result of the French Cabinet meeting which took place under Pétain's chairmanship. The German envoy in Vichy, Krugg von Nidda, wrote a commentary on this answer which was then transmitted to me by the German Chargé d'Affaires, Ambassador Schleier.

Re: 1.   'Dispatch.'

To the Bds., Paris.

Attention of S.S. Staff and Police Colonel Dr. Knochen, to be submitted to him personally at once.—Secret.

Re: *Present French Cabinet.*

Have just had a conversation with de Brinon in his hotel room. He informs me that to-day's Cabinet meeting was anything but pleasant. One felt that one had been put back into the period of the worst parliamentarism. The upshot of the Cabinet meeting, he stated, is that Laval will to-morrow morning hand Krugg von Nidda a note in which he will inform him that he will agree to the work of the German-French Commission which is to be appointed, but that he will in no event assume any obligation or even contemplate the possibility of sending any more French workers to work in Germany. De Brinon adds that Laval is, in fact, opposed to sending even a single French workman further to Germany.

De Brinon states that the Marshal is just as basically opposed to sending one more worker. De Brinon arrived in Vichy this afternoon at four o'clock and immediately called on the Marshal in order to try to influence him. He told me that he could do absolutely nothing, because the Marshal has already been influenced in the opposite direction by his entourage. A regular siege has been laid to the Marshal in order to make him inaccessible to any other opinion. He alleges that Ménétrel and Jardel have been particularly active along these lines.

I shall be arriving in Paris to-morrow about twelve o'clock, for a few hours, for a conference with VI. If you want to speak to me for a short time for any reason please transmit this message by telephone to VI N 1. I would then be at your disposal during the afternoon.

Delegation D. Dt. Pol. u EK. Vichy, TGB. No. 437/41.

Re: 2.

Translation of reply of the Head of the French Government: Having reported to the Marshal and the ministers, I am in a position to inform you of the French Government's reply to the inquiries which have been addressed to me through Gauleiter Sauckel.

1. The French Government declares that it agrees to the enrolment of one million workers from the civilians' sector and their allocation to the French factories which have been instructed to meet the new German orders placed with France.

2. It is impossible for the French Government to assume any obligation under which a definite contingent of workers is to be sent to Germany before 31 December.

However:

   (*a*) It confirms its decision to allow the 60,000 workers who represent the balance of the third recruiting campaign to leave within the very shortest time.
   (*b*) It promises to seek out those among the recruits in this third campaign who have defaulted or refused to work.
   (*c*) It declares itself in agreement with the joint German-French Commissions entrusted with ensuring the transfer provided for under Point No. 1, at the same time conducting a general inquiry into labour reserves.

At no time may this inquiry assume the form of an investigation which would be made with a view to new departures for Germany.

The results of this inquiry can serve as the basis for a further conference with Gauleiter Sauckel to be held at a later date.

In the meantime the measures provided for in paragraphs (*a*) and (*b*) will be continued.

As an illustration of the general state of opinion in Vichy, it has been reported to me that circles in contact with Pétain, who, in some peculiar manner, is said to be thoroughly informed only as to the English and American army communiqués, are openly stating that the collapse of Germany is imminent, so that the time for the French Government to make any further commitment towards Germany must now be considered over.

Further, Laval wishes to make it clear in political discussions with the Führer that France would now give Germany political assistance in peace negotiations, since Germany alone can no longer achieve victory. He wishes France, even though defeated, to be generously treated, as a great nation to be reckoned and negotiated with on broader grounds. I have rejected this argument and unequivocally pointed out our strength and unwavering intention to win the decisive final victory.

My Führer,

I have felt myself in duty bound to inform you at once in this report, openly and without reticence, of the general mental attitude and situation found in Paris. Please, however, rest assured that I shall do everything in order to achieve a positive success, if not with the French, then without them. Preparations for this are already well under way. I have postponed my departure until they are perfected. I am also uninterruptedly in contact with the German official departments and services here and, thanks to my urgent representations, entire unanimity exists amongst us.

I am convinced that you also, my Führer, will feel that it is preferable to look things squarely in the face now, as dispassionately as possible, and to act accordingly. A pleasant surprise would then be all the more welcome.

Always your obedient and grateful,

Paris, 9 August 1943.　　　　　　　　　Doc. HAA 021.
(Translated from the German.)

APPENDIX VI

This eleven-page report was sent secretly to Dr. Goebbels by Fernand de Brinon, on May 11th, 1943, and was discovered in the Goebbels archives in Berlin. This document, which formed part of the State's case against de Brinon, was not admitted as evidence, being considered too favourable to Pierre Laval.

Laval has known too many parliamentarians, and has worked with them too much to be able to rid himself of these political habits and friendships.

*** National-Socialism is foreign to his personal conception of life, undoubtedly much more foreign than it was in the case of M. Edouard Daladier.

When M. Laval assumed power again, he failed to make the necessary changes at a time when many people thought them possible. He merely rid himself of a certain number of individuals who had taken active part in the machinations of December 13th, 1940.***

*** In order really to understand the political situation in France it is necessary to know the character and peculiarities of the Marshal, Chief of the French State, and of President Laval, Chief of the Government; and it is also necessary to know what places them in opposition to each other. Although both are of peasant origin, they are very different. The Marshal is a soldier, whose fame rests on his military valour and his personal appearance. He has always despised politicians even when he was interested in politics himself. He was a cabinet member in the Doumergue Government and—before the defeat of France—in the Reynaud Government. In each case he commented ironically (this is one of his characteristic traits) on his colleagues at the centre of government, and in this way even encouraged those opposed to the regime.***

*** Raised to power by the signing of the armistice and the confusion following the defeat, Marshal Pétain, who owed his post to the parliamentary action of M. Laval, nevertheless never gave the latter any recognition.***

*** The Marshal desires a sort of conservative revolution, which M. Laval, naturally, abhors, but this does not mean that M. Laval would like a National-Socialist revolution. Since the beginning of his career in public life, which started with socialism, he has consistently retained his taste for pacifism, which fills the Marshal with horror.

The Marshal, whose heart does not go out to parliamentarians and the beneficiaries of the old regime, thinks M. Laval supports and protects too many of the latter. He also thinks too many free-masons, whom (like so many military men of his party) he distrusts, still hold important posts in the machinery of government. In his eyes Admiral Platon, in whom he placed great confidence, seemed to be against free-masonry, and Admiral Platon did not hesitate to declare his opposition to M. Laval, and his group, on that subject. Therein lies the main reason for the present resentment felt by the Chief of State towards the Prime Minister and for the dis-unity on the subject of domestic policy which the Marshal exhibits on every occasion and which he wanted to emphasise in his answer to the Führer's last letter.***

*** In examining certain details it is not hard to find that, in the press and on the radio, the notorious adversaries of Franco-German collaboration continue their work; that many administrative posts, a large number of Prefectures and numerous municipalities, are held by tolerated enemies, by partisans of the old regime, and that the Government permits a large section of the clergy to convey a hostile attitude through their religious instruction and sermons.

In each of these domains a few severe admonitions would suffice to bring each one back into line, but these admonitions are never given. Perhaps because daily anxieties prevent thinking of them, or because, on the one hand, criticism on the part of the Marshal is feared, or, on the other, opposition on the part of friends of the Prime Minister.

In this way, public opinion is allowed to drift and becomes susceptible to Anglo-Saxon propaganda.

*** It is inexplicable that the only strong measure taken after M. Laval's return from Berchtesgaden, where he had been urged to finish with his political adversaries, consisted in sending Admiral Platon, one of the few higher officers who had consistently manifested hostile sentiments towards the Soviets, England and America, to residence under surveillance.

*** How can one understand letting prisoners of war with anti-German sentiments leave their camps, when designated by men in confidential posts and known to be partisans of de Gaulle or Giraud, while other prisoners of war, adept enthusiasts for the reconciliation with Germany, are held in the same camps? Only those prisoners of war should be permitted to leave camp who are themselves—or whose French relatives are—in favour of an understanding with Germany and against Bolshevism. Such prisoners might become the best propaganda agents.

And, to cite one last example, how can one explain that, in a propaganda field as important as the cinema, persons who before the outbreak of war advocated going to war and who continue to hold anti-German opinions, like M. Chanon, should be placed by the Prime Minister at the head of an organisation as large as the Societé Gaumont?

I feel myself obligated to mention these facts, because they seriously interfere with the present situation.

APPENDIX VII

MANIFESTO AGAINST PIERRE LAVAL'S POLICY OF "NEUTRALITY", JULY 5TH, 1944

Joint Declaration on the Political Situation.

The assassination of Philippe Henriot brutally destroys our national propaganda in the form in which it most interfered with the Allies. His death is an irreparable loss to France, a serious defeat for the Government, which has thus lost the spokesman who could give daily expression to its political thought.

This misfortune comes at the exact moment when the general situation is unfavourable to the Government. The Anglo-American landing, the fall of Cherbourg, the imminence of further landings, the progress of the Russian offensive, the crises in supplies and transportation, have created an atmosphere extremely propitious to the anarchy organised by the Allies on our soil.

Doubtless some time will elapse before the Germans offer the Anglo-Saxons a decisive battle. Until then public opinion will daily become more certain that Germany has lost the war, and the internal situation will steadily become worse. We are on the eve of the great test of strength between the Government—responsible for order and accountable for a policy it has not officially disclaimed—and the 'Resistance', relying on the popular masses, which have been profoundly influenced by Allied propaganda.

The object of the 'Resistance' is doubtless not so much the spectacular seizure of power as the obliteration of what remains of an organised State. Nevertheless one must foresee that the active participation of Communist forces which have, until now, been held in reserve, will weigh very heavily in the fate of the French nation.

This struggle is beginning under the worst conditions. On one side we have a determined will and the conviction of power—on the other, purely defensive governmental action, undermined by internal doubts and hesitancy.

Everyone is now aware of the Administration's weakness. The boldness and strength of the army of disorder increases accordingly. Rightly or wrongly, the latest declarations of the Chief of State, Marshal Pétain, and the Prime Minister, Pierre Laval, have been unanimously interpreted as signs of profound uneasiness. There is not a journalist, a militant partisan, and certainly no civil servant who does not feel, though somewhat confusedly, that the Government is fascinated and paralysed by the idea of an approaching Anglo-American taking-over in France. Such an atmosphere can only precipitate the disintegration of the French State.

To imagine the Government capable of surviving the approaching collapse is to delude oneself profoundly. In any case, such survival, guaranteed only by German considerations of opportunism, will end with German victory or German defeat, in case of a defeat. Whatever promises for the future may have been given by the Anglo-Americans to certain members of the Vichy government, they will become worthless on the day when, with France in complete anarchy, the whole world will come to realise the professional incompetence of the men who for four years have presided over the administration of this country.

This internal anarchy must be stopped at once. The ills are political and result from the failure of the Government to define France's choice in this world-conflict and to state the civic duties which should be the inevitable consequences of that choice. Precept and example would prove strength, faith and intelligence to be on the side of the Government and not on the side of its adversaries. Thousands of civil servants, millions of Frenchmen, will rally around Authority when it is manifested. The treason of some or the delusions of others are merely due to the failure of those who should command.

If it is clear that the policy advocated in 1940, re-affirmed and re-enforced today, is the only conceivable one, it must be concluded that no government whatever can now hold France together except by affirming its power within the framework of that policy.

The essential steps to be taken are few to begin with:

1. As to declarations—An unequivocal and binding declaration of policy by the Government.

2. Return of the Government to Paris.

3. Inclusion in the Government of dependable persons.

4. Reform of the inner functioning of the Council of Ministers (Cabinet), which should be compelled to deliberate upon, and express its views on, matters of general policy.

5. Severe sanctions, going as far as capital punishment, against all whose actions encourage civil war or compromise the position of France in Europe.

Only at such a cost can the French State be revived. Only at such a cost will the Reich find a France at her side capable of covering with her the last stretch of the road to the victory of Europe.

Unless these conditions are met, Germany will have to finish the war dragging the weight of a France plunged into chaos.

(Following is the list of signatories)

The attached declaration has been signed by:

Abel Bonnard   Fernand de Brinon
Jean Bichelonne   Marcel Déat

Also signed by

Admiral Platon	Former Minister
Benoist-Méchin	Former Minister
Jean Luchaire	President of the Newspaper Syndicate
General Duchêne	
Jacques Doriot	President of the 'Parti Populaire Français' Ex-Major General of the anti-Soviet Expeditionary Forces
General Bineau	Former Chief of Staff of Marshal Pétain
George Claude	Industrialist
René Dommange	Former Member of Parliament
Xavier de Magallon	Former Member of Parliament

The following authors, journalists and militants signed also:

Georges Albertini	Secretary General of the 'Rassemblement National Populaire'
Michel Alerme	Editor of the 'Petit Parisien'
Henri Barbé	Member of the Action Committee of the Restaurants Communautairs
Victor Barthélémy	Secretary General of the 'Parti Populaire Français'
Jean Bérard	
Alphonse de Chateaubriant	Editor of 'La Gerbe'
Lucien Combelle	Editor of 'Révolution Nationale'
P. A. Cousteau	Managing Editor of 'Paris-Soir'
Guy Crouzet	Managing Editor of 'Nouveaux Temps'
Georges Guilbaud	Editor of 'l'Echo de la France'
Drieux La Rochelle	
Henri Lèbre	Editor of 'Cri du Peuple'
Charles Lesca	Editor 'Je suis Partout'
Jacques de Lesdain	Editor 'l'Illustration'
Lucien Rebatet	
General Mangeot	Military correspondent of 'Nouveaux Temps'
Jacques Roujon	Editor of 'Petit Parisien'
Dominique Sordet	Editor 'l'Inter-France'
Georges Suarez	Editor of 'Aujourdhui'

Other signatures are being collected.

APPENDIX VIII

(Secret Minutes.)

CABINET MEETING, WEDNESDAY, JULY 12, 1944, 4 P.M.

All Secretaries and Undersecretaries of State are present except M. Marcel Déat.*

[PIERRE LAVAL] . . . Gentlemen, I wish to apologise for making you come on such short notice but circumstances compelled me to do so—I was informed yesterday morning of a visit Admiral Platon ** made to the Marshal. Among other things the Admiral told the Marshal all the members of the Government were about to resign with the exception of Cathala and Grasset. I immediately telephoned M. de Brinon and M. Bichelonne, who told me this was not true. Then I told M. de Brinon to ask all Cabinet members to attend this meeting in Vichy to-day, making it very clear that all those who did not attend would be considered by me as having resigned.

M. Déat replied that when he came into the Government it had been agreed he need never come to Vichy. M. Déat also gave me his word of honour that he would no longer write in the *Oeuvre* except once a week and on non-political subjects. He did not keep his promise. I also though that when entering the Government he was implicitly undertaking to refrain from destroying the Government's authority—and only a few minutes ago this manifesto [Pierre Laval points to a document before him] was brought to me. It bears the signatures of Bonnard,

* Marcel Déat represented, with de Brinon, the extreme collaborationist parties in the Vichy Government.

** Also a member of the extreme collaborationist parties, whom Laval had forced to resign from the Government a few months before.

Bichelonne, Brinon, Déat, and those of many other personalities . . .

[DE BRINON] It is true that I approved, with slight reservations, the ideas expressed in this document. . . .

[PIERRE LAVAL] I will read it to you. [Pierre Laval reads the manifesto, and adds] . . .

It is obvious that those who signed this document do not agree with my statement of June 6.* They wish to have the Government resort to certain 'acts', certain 'gestures'. May I ask, which ones? They want the Government to be 'strengthened'. May I inquire by whose coöperation?

[M. de Brinon then explains how Pierre Laval's attitude in the Henriot and Mandel affairs has produced a bad impression on the collaborationist and German circles in Paris . . .]

[PIERRE LAVAL . . . striking the table with his fist . . .] I will not permit certain things to be said here. A few days ago, I was advised by the German embassy that Léon Blum, Paul Reynaud and Mandel were to be delivered to the French Government to serve as hostages and be shot in the event Colonel Magnien, head of the Tricolour Legion, who has been sentenced to death at Algiers, was executed. I told Abetz that I indignantly refused. I added that such a measure constituted a violation of the laws of war and might be the prelude to civil war in France. I said that nothing could be more contrary to my character. That I had no blood on my hands and wanted none. . . .

M. Mandel was delivered by the German authorities to M. Baillet, Director of the Penitentiary Administration. . . . He did not, for reasons of security, want to keep him at the Santé Prison and Mandel was taken into custody by the militia. You know the rest. The same thing happened to Jean Zay, a few days ago. Two crimes

* Pierre Laval had urged the people on D-day to take a passive attitude and to adhere to The Hague conventions.

such as these are too much. I want those here who might
be of an opposite opinion to say so. . . .

[No one asks to speak.]

. . . I therefore wish to put on record that the Cabinet
is unanimous in its refusal to accept any delivery of hostages.

[M. GABOLDE, Minister of Justice] An investigation has just
been commenced. Mandel's body, riddled by six bullets,
was taken to the police at Bonnières near Versailles. . . .

[PIERRE LAVAL] I was going to ask you to make an investigation . . .

Now, the authors of the manifesto want the Government to return to Paris. Déat asked me the same thing,
a few days ago. The Diplomatic Corps is here in Vichy.
Its presence is a symbol of French Sovereignty. The legal
seat of the Government is Vichy. Furthermore, it is not
in our power to create the political conditions necessary for
the Government's return to Paris. The Germans failed to
create them. These conditions relate to press censorship
and, when I see that all the newspaper editors have signed
this manifesto, I realise even more the necessity for the
Government to have the right of control.

I know M. Déat complained to the German Ambassador that political issues were never discussed at our Cabinet meetings. I notice that on the one occasion when I
am discussing these questions he is not here. . . . In
reading the manifesto, I wonder whether the authors would
like to make speeches of this type [Pierre Laval points
to the document] at Cabinet meetings. In reading this
document, I notice that the one essential task of the Government, that of feeding the people, is not even mentioned. If I understand the meaning of this paper, one
thing is certain and clear as day: I must go—I must be
replaced. If times were different I should merely go but,
when I read papers like these, I am not at all convinced
that it would be the proper thing to do. The Government

should be strengthened, the paper goes on to say.—By whose presence? Admiral Platon?—Well, I will give you an example of Admiral Platon's style.—He forgets that letters are censored and here is what he wrote to his brother a few days ago [Pierre Laval reads from letter]:

'I think it is shocking that the head of the Government tells us that we are not in this war. Such a man deserves not to be shot but to be hanged, and he will be.'

M. Platon is a fine man. He played a heroic role at Dunkirk, but it would be better if he did not play politics. M. Platon, like many other arch-collaborationists, devotes lots of thinking to Europe but seldom speaks of France. I am convinced that the United States and Great Britain alone will not be able to prevent Communism from taking over Europe. I have a long political experience behind me and will not accept lessons from the persons who signed this paper. I am concerned only about France. I was born here and wish to die here and I will never abandon my country.

On the day of the Allied landing, 6 June, I broadcast a statement which is challenged to-day. I said: 'France is not in this war.' Some want France to enter the war on Germany's side. I ask you: With what arms? M. Déat states he is not neutral? If that is so, why doesn't he just enlist. He wants to see Frenchmen fight alongside Germans but fails to realise that this would lead to civil war. I wish here once again to reaffirm my position:

They say Pierre Laval is neutral, which is intolerable, and Platon adds 'he must be hanged'. I am going to ask you a question: Is there anyone here who believes that France can follow a policy different from mine?

[A. BONNARD] Considering the present condition of France, I would say no but, later on, action will have to be taken through small organised groups to lead the unorganised masses.

[PIERRE LAVAL] What do you mean? When you refer to

small organised groups do you refer to the political parties paid by the German Government? These are not French parties. Their so-called groups for social peace are nothing but bodies of denunciation. Do you seriously believe you are going to revive France with these groups? Déat must put an end to his activity—he must resign or take my place. I can no longer work with him. If he comes to power, it will just mean catastrophe and civil war. In order to end this discussion I ask you: Are you in complete agreement with the line of policy expressed in my statement of 6 June?

[. . . Silence . . .]

[Pierre Laval] I take this to mean that you all agree.

APPENDIX IX

Pierre Laval.—But the Reich wants Central Europe—that is as clear as day, and we are doing nothing to prevent it. And you offer me newspaper articles! A terrible drama is being played out concerning our country, and France says nothing because she is too comfortable.

The Minister of Foreign Affairs, M. Georges Bonnet: What would you do in my place?

Pierre Laval: I should get out. We are all Frenchmen here and I speak frankly: What is going on is abominable. It makes my blood boil to see the situation France has got herself into. Germany, after having lost the war, to-day possesses territories greater than those of 1914. The Austro-Hungarian Empire has been destroyed. The Protestants—I can speak frankly here—did not want this Catholic Empire maintained in the centre of Europe and evil forces combined to break up this important group of countries which, even after the Allied victory, constituted a counterpoise to German power. The evil is done and to-day we see the octopus spreading its tentacles. . . . M. Bachelet presented the problem correctly when he said: 'If it is true that Hitler and Mussolini are in agreement we shall soon receive a challenge. Then we must defend ourselves and we shall be able to rely,' M. Bachelet said, 'on the allies that we have.' I fear though, that in listing the number of our allies, M. Bachelet shows himself too generous towards France, because the small countries of Central Europe will be afraid. There is but one way of preventing Hitler from seizing Europe and that is, with Rome, Belgrade, Budapest, Warsaw, Bucharest, and Moscow, to forge a chain around Germany, extending from

London to Paris. Otherwise, Germany will win. I am repeating a figure of speech that I employed at Stresa in even more forcible terms when I talked to Mr. Macdonald. . . .

M. Bachelet, are you and your friends capable of understanding that the interests of France should come before those of our political parties, that if political passion has blinded us to the extent of tearing up the Franco-Italian treaties, to-day it is the duty of all Frenchmen to unite and to checkmate Germany?

I demand that the Government find the solution. One solution is impossible and that is to permit Germany to continue what she is now doing. I had the honour of directing, for some months, France's foreign policy. Since then I have seen fall away, one by one, all the advantages of the Versailles Treaty, but to-day it is a question of territories which, one after another, are being added to Germany. I say that this must stop or else in a few days or it may be a few months French blood will run and hundreds of thousands of wooden crosses will be scattered throughout our cemeteries. To prevent it, there is still one attempt that can be made, only one. . . .

On 23 March—before the Czechoslovakian affair—M. Paul Boncour was Minister of Foreign Affairs; he seemed to understand, or at least he said he did, that Italy would end by coming back into the Anglo-French orbit, and I told him that I was glad to hear him say so, but I added that it seemed to me absolutely imperative that her return should be hastened. In fact, these are the terms I used: 'I can see no other way of saving our honour, of defending our interests, and of safeguarding peace.'

This was not done. As for our honour, we know what happened to it at Munich. We know what was done that evening, when those who had led France to Munich went to salute, beneath the Arc de Triomphe, the unknown soldier who died for France in the trenches. . . .

You see in what condition the interests of our country find themselves to-day.

What was true on 23 March is even more true to-day. It was difficult at that time, on account of our internal political situation and our internal dissensions, to apply the policy of agreement with Italy which I recommended. It is still more difficult to-day, and still because of our domestic politics. All the same, do we desire to accomplish anything? Do we, at least, wish to try?

I ask you to reopen conversations with Italy. Do you believe that she is not interested in this problem, and that she does not know that as soon as Germany becomes really powerful her turn will come?

Charlemagne of olden times was a great man, a very great fellow indeed, but he believed in God. To-day, Charlemagne no longer believes in anything; he himself is God. For that, there is no precedent in history. You will look in vain through the textbooks of our schools and those of our universities for events like those of to-day. Do you not feel that there is something which should drive you to unite with all those who may become Hitler's victims?

Will you try? If so, there is a chance of preserving peace. If not, you risk precipitating your country into a terrible and tragic adventure such as has never before been known.

I have presented the problem. I apologise for having been over-eloquent. I should have been much more eloquent had I been able to express all I feel.

Ah! If Hitler could only imagine—but he does imagine it— all that is going on in Paris, these hearings of the Minister of Foreign Affairs at the Chamber and at the Senate where, with great detail, they explain to us how Germany seized Czechoslovakia. How he must laugh! If he knew how ashamed I feel, how I blush to the roots of my hair, when I recall before you the conversation, which lasted four hours, in a small hotel room at Cracow, with Goering. At that time it was Goering who reproached me for all the measures we were taking to encircle Germany. He reproached me because France was always found in every combination directed against Germany. And to-day it is Hitler's old adversaries, the anti-Nazis and the anti-Fascists, all the irreconcilable foes of the regimes of force, who are making Hitler's bed for him and assuring his triumph.

I beg you, let's wake up. We all have, to a greater or lesser degree, a responsibility, for we are all representatives of our country. So, if I affirm that it is possible to reach an understanding with Mussolini, will you try? If you do not, you are criminals and you commit against your country the greatest crime of high treason ever yet committed.

The Minister of Foreign Affairs: M. Pierre Laval believes that at the present moment it is possible to negotiate with Italy?

Pierre Laval: I regard it as indispensable. Possible, you ask? That depends on Mussolini and on yourself. But I fear that, given the line of policy you are pursuing towards him, it will be terribly difficult for you.

The day you wish to succeed in reaching an agreement with Mussolini you must know before beginning the negotiations exactly what he is after. You must inform yourself of that and it must be he who demands and not you who offer, for he needs a moral success in the eyes of his people. The fundamental grievance that he and all Italians have against us is that to-day Germany is on the Brenner Pass. Therefore it is essential—and I repeat this forcefully—that we should reach an understanding with Italy. The difficulty is to know whether you really want it. And on that point I am astonished at the questions which are being asked: 'Do you think,' say some of you, 'that Parliament will be pleased?' What does that matter to me? Do you not think that this Parliament has done enough harm to France and that Hitler is not already grateful enough to it? The only thing which counts is the interests of France, and it is those interests that you are defending. Have the courage to take this attitude and the deputies will save themselves like rabbits the day they learn that the people are with you. For the people, who are being deceived, who are being lied to, will be with us when they are convinced that you are defending solely the interests of the nation. I know of no sadder session than the present one and yet nobody would think it from your behaviour.

In order not to stare at me in rage, Mr. Minister, you are shifting your gaze to the tapestry behind you. How much better it would be if, in the place of that tapestry, there had been a map. They made fun of me when I asked for one. If you had a map of Europe in front of you, Mr. Minister, where you could see how Germany is spreading out every day, then you would understand what your duty is. You would realise that your agreements with Yugoslavia and Poland, your relations with Hungary, all count for little or nothing if you are not in accord with Italy. I ask you, Mr. Minister, do you want an agreement with Rome? Perhaps you will tell me, as we go out: 'I am willing to make the effort but I am not alone,' and perhaps your chief * will also tell me, as he did when I urged him to send a representative to Burgos: 'I should risk losing twenty or thirty radical votes.' Well, if that is the point which you've reached, I come back to what I said before—'Get out.'

* Reference is made here to M. Daladier, President of the Council of Ministers.

APPENDIX X (a)

THE LAST PAGE WRITTEN BY PIERRE LAVAL

à mes avocats pour les informer
à mes bourreaux pour leur répondre　　　　*15 octobre 1945*

Je n'ai maintenant aucun doute sur le sort qui m'attend.

Le général de Gaulle n'a pas hésité pas à ordonner mon assassinat. Ce n'est pas une exécution, puisque l'arrêt qui me frappe n'est-il pas un jugement. On m'a fermé la bouche à l'audience, on veut éteindre ma voix pour toujours — Ainsi on ne redoutera plus mes déclarations — Il n'est pas nécessaire que la France connaisse son histoire. On ne veut pas surtout qu'elle connaisse les responsables de nos malheurs —

J'ai adressé un appel suprême à deux hommes politiques dont j'ai sauvé la vie — à Léon Blum et à Paul Reynaud — Tout a été vain.

Je n'accepte pas le verdict — Je n'accepte pas la souillure d'une exécution puisqu'il s'agit d'un meurtre. J'entends mourir à ma manière par le poison comme les Romains — C'est mon dernier acte pour protester contre la sauvagerie — Je vais utiliser le petit paquet de graines qu'aucune fouille n'a pas découvert — le poison a voyagé — puis s'il ne sera pas éventé — car il a été souvent changé de refuge — Ma grosse pelisse dans sa poche intérieure lui fut souvent hospitalière — et ma serviette qui en respecta toujours l'accueillit parfois quand il était mieux empaqueté —

Des soldats fusillent par devoir, mais aujourd'hui leur devoir est redoutable. On les oblige à accomplir un meurtre. Grâce à moi ils ne seront pas les complices même involontaires de ceux qui là haut leur ont ordonné mon assassinat. Ils n'auront pas à tirer sur un homme qui doit mourir parce qu'il a trop aimé sa patrie —

Je demande qu'on me laisse mon foulard tricolore. Je désire le garder pour le grand voyage.

On aura réussi à éteindre ma voix pour toujours mais mon esprit renaîtra plus vivant et plus fort — J'adresse mon dernier salut à la France que j'ai servie. Ma dernière pensée est pour elle.

Pierre Laval

APPENDIX X (b)

To My Lawyers, to inform them.

To My Torturers, that they may be answered.

I have no more doubt about the fate awaiting me. General de Gaulle does not hesitate to order my assassination.

It is not an execution, since the order against me is not a judgment. They sealed my mouth at the trial; now they wish to silence my voice forever. Thus they will no longer need to fear my statements; it is not necessary that France should know her own history. Above all, they do not want her to know who are responsible for her misfortunes.

I addressed a supreme appeal to two statesmen, both of whose lives I saved: Léon Blum and Paul Reynaud. It was useless.

I do not accept the sentence. I do not accept the stigma of execution; it is murder. I intend to die in my own way, by poison, like the Romans. This is my final act of protest against savagery. I shall use the little packet of capsules which no search has discovered. This poison has travelled: I hope it will not have lost its strength for it has often had to change its hiding-place. The inside pocket of my fur coat sheltered it and my brief-case, which was always respected, sometimes received the packet when it was better wrapped.

To execute is the duty of soldiers but to-day their duty is questionable. They are obliged to commit a murder. Thanks to me they will not be the accomplices, even involuntarily, of those who, from their very high positions, have ordered my assassination. They will not have to fire on a man who must die because he loved his country too much.

I ask that my tricolour scarf be left with me. I want to keep it for the long journey.

They will succeed in silencing my voice for ever, but my spirit will be reborn, more alive and stronger.

I give my last salute to the France that I have served. My last thought is for her.

PIERRE LAVAL.

APPENDIX XI

FROM THE GOEBBELS DIARIES, NOVEMBER 17, 1943 AND
NOVEMBER 21, 1943

'Rather disagreeable developments are observable in
France. Laval keeps hesitating. It's not quite clear whether
he is delaying from apathy or intrigue. Certainly Pétain is
very much dissatisfied and would like to get rid of him. That
is why he has been wanting to regulate the question of his
succession anew and to announce the change in a broadcast.
However, at the last moment, German censorship prevented
the speech. Now both Pétain and Laval have gone in for
watchful waiting. Both, in their innermost hearts, are quite
naturally opposed to the Reich and its interests. We therefore cannot trust them across the street. Pétain is nursing the
wishful dream that France may be called upon to establish
peace between Germany and the Western Powers!

'Although Pétain has thus far given no indication of any
intention to resign, he is nevertheless very much offended
and blames the German occupation authorities for the failure
of his plan. Laval, following his old tactics, has kept out of
the conflict. His attitude towards Pétain and ourselves is less
clear than ever.'

APPENDIX XII

. . . 'As soon as Spain takes part in the war,' the Fuehrer added, 'Gibralter will be occupied and a bridgehead established towards Morocco'. (I am here merely summing up what was said with a great abundance of detail). 'I will not sacrifice a true friend to a country like France, which for three centuries has been our irreconcilable enemy, for I do not at all believe in France's friendship and I know that there is really no difference between Pétain, Laval, Weygand and de Gaulle: they appear to be at odds; actually, they are working, as is quite natural, in complete accord' . . .

See, also, in document found in the Palais de Chigi's archives (Italian Ministry of Foreign Affairs), text of a telegram sent by Dino Alfieri, the Italian Ambassador to Berlin, on August 5, 1942, to his Minister of Foreign Affairs, Count Ciano, reporting the conversation that he had had, on that day, with Hitler at Berditchev (Hitler's headquarters on the Russian front). Alfieri reports what Hitler said to him about Laval:

'Again, even to-day, you may note that at heart a common tie links de Gaulle and Laval; the former is simply trying to obtain by force what the latter seeks to achieve through guile.'

239

APPENDIX XIII

Last Question and Answer of the Deposition of Hans Richard Hemmen (Von Ribbentrop's Personal Representative in Paris for All Economic and Financial Questions) from the Transcript of the Nürnberg Records

By Dr. Pelckmann:

Q. And I put to you the categorical question whether, already at that time—during the entire time of the occupation—this impression was predominant with all the German agencies, the impression that Laval tried to make the best of the situation in which he found himself and to act in the best interests of his country? Is that correct?

A. We intermediaries were convinced of the fact that Laval, with his great mental superiority, his tremendous knowledge, his amazing skill, and also, his ability to approach his opponent from the human side, would reduce to a fraction all the demands made upon him and that he would probably be able to defer the execution of such demands.

Dr. Pelckmann: Thank you. No further questions.